The United States of Bankruptcy

If America were a company, the board of directors and management would be fired and probably even in jail.

—Bill Glynn

The United States of Bankruptcy

20 Ideas to Save the American Way of Life

Bill Glynn

FRANKLIN GREEN
PUBLISHING

Published by
Franklin Green Publishing
500 Wilson Pike Circle, Suite 100
Brentwood, Tennessee 37027
www.franklingreenpublishing.com

ISBN 978-0-9826387-50

For information about bulk purchases or licensing of *The United States of Bankruptcy,* please contact Franklin Green Publishing.

Printed in the United States of America

Trust: a firm reliance on the integrity, ability, or character of a person or thing.

Confidence: trust or faith in a person or thing.

Ask yourself this...

Do you think politicians can actually manage our money?

Do you trust the motivations of your elected officials?

Do you think elections are nothing more than consumer advertising and branding?

Do you trust large corporations?

Do you trust Wall Street?

Do you trust the Chinese to control your future?

Do you feel your job is secure?

Do you think your money is safe?

Do you trust health insurance companies?

If you have answered no to any or all of these questions, you are not alone.

If you are looking for ideas to solve these problems within our country, then read on. This is your country, but only if you make it so.

CONTENTS

The United States of Bankruptcy

INTRODUCTION

WE HAVE TO FACE the fact that our nation is BANKRUPT! Financially, spiritually, and socially! Our cities and states are crumbling. Hopelessness is everywhere. We have created a permanent social underclass; our family values, morals, and spiritual compass are spinning like instruments in the Bermuda Triangle. There is disintegration of our society from within by urban hip-hop, liberal television, biased publications and media, waste and abuse in Washington, and an economic disaster of which we have only seen the beginning.

The United States government and its leaders have bankrupted our nation. Worse, our leaders have forfeited our national sovereignty to the hands of foreign nations who own our debt and those we depend on to keep buying more. It is appalling. Our government and business leaders have gone way too far, and "We the people" have to pay and pay and pay for their mistakes.

Even worse, we have been trained to think and are often told we live in a democracy. In fact, the United States is a republic where the people empower our elected officials who are supposed to be looking out for the best interests of our nation. But, frankly, none of our perceptions are true. Political power is won or lost during elections, and the fact that billions of dollars are spent during every election cycle to give you your opinion is at best a corruption of the system. The media is the most powerful weapon of the twenty-first century, and the political machines use it to massively influence the results of elections. Elections are nothing more than consumer branding led by commercials designed for us to buy a political product, and if it didn't work to pull us along by the nose, then nobody would spend a penny on it. So even power in America is for sale—and it is very much so—hence the tens of billions of dollars spent annually for lobbying and advertising about people, issues, and laws. So money buys power, and those with more money are way more likely to be elected and definitely very able to influence the laws and the government in their favor. So the truth is that we live in an oligarchy, ruled by the few—the rich and powerful—where an individual's ability to effect any change in this nation has been lost.

I.O.U.S.A.—a movie and short book—recently examined America's spiraling national debt and presented interviews from America's most successful and brightest executives, including Alan Greenspan, Pete Peterson, and Warren Buffet. You need to read it or get the movie—it will have a dramatic impact on you. The United States is now burdened with $13 trillion in debt, a forthcoming federal deficit of at least $3 trillion over just the next few years, $20 trillion in debt projected by the end of the decade, and a proposed $1 trillion Health-Caid overhaul. In 2008 the United States paid and/or rolled over $451 billion ($212 billion accrued as a noncash interest expense for intragovernmental debt, primarily the Social Security Trust Fund—more IOUs) in just interest payments on our debt, and in 2009 $383 billion. Our government has over $100 trillion of unfunded liabilities to make sure programs like Social Security, Medicare, Medicaid, and others can survive. America is on the verge of bankruptcy, if not already, and *I.O.U.S.A.* paints a grave picture of these facts.

As a shareholder of this nation, I want answers and I demand solutions to protect our way of life. If we allow the government to do more of the same, we will lose more international confidence in our economy than we have already, and we will be cut off from those nations buying our debt and keeping the United States from bankruptcy right now. As bleak as all this sounds, I believe solutions can be brought to the political process. Hopefully someone will listen to reason before it is too late.

In this short book I address many sore subjects that America must overcome in order to keep our society and way of life going. Our nation suffers from a cancer, metastasizing from the inside, which is exactly how Rome fell! Political inaction, incompetence, and the continued disintegration of our society ensure that America will follow suit.

One thing for certain is that history repeats. We do not want history repeating on us!

—Bill Glynn

1

The Silver Bullet

10 Percent Solution

I have spent the last two years on talk radio promoting the solutions in this book (most of this was written between twelve and twenty-four months ago) to help turn around our nation's woes, including the 10 percent solution as an easy-to-understand cure for the American debt catastrophe. Now I want to share the broad strokes with you.

In essence, the 10 percent solution proposal would require by law that 10 percent of the *fully* invested portfolios of pensions, Union Taft Hartley, 401(k)s, endowments, and corporate investments that combined are valued at over $30 trillion (two years ago it was more) and professionally managed (not our individual stock accounts) be reallocated into a single pooled investment vehicle to serve as the U.S. Debt Fund. This fund would be managed by our nation's most successful businesspeople. In fact, those institutions have to invest 100 percent of the money under management for you and me and already hold some treasuries and other fixed income investments, cash, and cash equivalents in the portfolios.

I am simply proposing that the institutional ownership of government debt by American money managers should be temporarily increased by 10 percent more than what it already is. The allocation of these funds into this debt fund would provide the requisite capital needed to buy back almost all of America's foreign debt in the fund's first year and put ownership of America back in American hands. As a law the 10 percent solution would have a limited shelf life of five to seven years (not permanent), or however long it takes to acquire and retire all U.S. debt (not just foreign) under this investment strategy.

Yes, initially this would drain money out of the stock market to meet the necessary cash requirements to invest in the fund. But facing bankruptcy—and we are—is far worse than a temporary equity and debt market issue. In fact, I expect that if the United States had a plan to buy back its debt and a means to retire it, the U.S. markets and America would become a great investment again, rise by far more than 10 percent, and the world would invest huge sums of money here because of renewed confidence in us.

In the first year the fund would have almost $3 trillion or more (10 percent of the $30 trillion + under professional management). A requirement is that 100 percent of the fund's money must be used initially to buy back U.S. foreign debt. Second, the fund would buy some of the hoards of currency recently minted to save the dollar from devaluation and protect against imminent inflation. Then funds would be used to shore up the federal interagency (Social Security, Medicare, Medicaid, and a host of others) ownership, which represents about 50 percent of the nation's debt (I mean IOUs) in order to quickly bring the country back from the brink of bankruptcy. Essential to this plan, and likely its political downfall, is that no political machine would ever have direct ties to this fund, so that it would remain a pure investment for acquiring national debt. The fund would never be used to perpetuate more of the government waste that got us here in the first place. I have heard over the last two years that the government can't do this or force it on the financial investment community! The government can't intervene into this system. OH, REALLY! What the heck just happened, or have I been watching the news channel from the Land of Misfit Toys?

Liberation Day! The Day America Freed Itself from the Grips of Foreign Nations

If this plan is implemented, institutions in the United States will have bought back almost all U.S. foreign debt and our sovereignty in the first year, but the government will still have to repay the investment. To do so, a large investment from the pool would be used to buy zero coupon bonds (without any current tax payments of course—and also not government STRIPS—largely corporation's zeros if used) or other instruments (like fixed income or insurance) to guarantee over a period of time that all monies will be repaid at the end of the investment by using the very money from the fund itself. The 10 percent increase in allocations and initial effect of pulling money into the fund from the market would also get shored up fast by re-injecting investment dollars into the market. The money raised and invested would work for the fund, and the government can shield itself from having to borrow more money later to repay it! For example, zero coupon bonds are bought at a discount—say two hundred dollars—and could mature to one thousand dollars at the end of the investment period. If the money invested in the U.S. Debt Fund is *guaranteed* to be paid back (no IOUs), a very low interest rate on the money invested in the fund is feasible. I strongly believe this would have a huge positive impact on the U.S. economy, and I expect the stock market would rise by far more than 10 percent.

We all know that when companies buy back their debt, retire it early, or purchase their own stock, it is a tremendous show of strength and confidence. At this time in history this has never been more necessary, as the world has lost confidence in America as a good investment. The river will run dry; it is just a matter of when.

Economy Bonds

How do we save the economy while transforming our credit-addicted nation back into a savings nation? My proposal to turn this tide is to allow Americans to buy economy bonds. Similar to war bonds—and make no mistake we are under the constant threat of economic war—economy bonds should be sold to everyone at every level of society, with all proceeds going to retire the national debt. The bonds should be tax free and become part of an individual investment program aimed at strengthening the economy by incentivizing Americans to invest in their nation, encouraging Americans to become savers instead of borrowers, and finally creating supplemental accounts to reinforce Social Security. In addition, I suggest 5 percent of all personal taxes (that is, if we don't smartly abolish income taxes) be swapped for the bonds each year to give Americans ownership in our country. And instead of sending a large portion of the other 50 percent that don't pay taxes a refund check, they would get a bond. As a result, Americans will have savings accounts, and the government can still use the proceeds without depleting tax revenue and borrowing more, just to send hundreds of billions of dollars to people who don't pay taxes. When Japan's financial institutions failed in the 1990s, Japan was rescued by the fact that she was a savings nation. America is not a savings nation. This major fact will perpetuate our financial crisis, and it will surely cause huge problems in the future if we do not solve it.

Credit Bureaus

America is a consumption economy. If consumers can't or won't buy products, goods, and services, every sector and every business will continue to suffer.

The last twenty-plus years of American economic growth were largely fueled by consumers using credit to buy goods and services. Now, many consumers are in rehab for credit addiction and will continue to be in rehab for many years. The credit transformation in America and around the world can no longer support all of the businesses that need consumers to buy things and won't allow many businesses to use credit to help their businesses to survive.

I believe the credit bureaus need to be tweaked during this economic crisis to weigh the last eighteen months and next eighteen months differently. You want to provide relief immediately? You want to reduce anxiety and hopelessness and increase consumer confidence? Then allow people to get access to decent loans and relieve the stress on families just trying to get by and pay their bills. If Americans cannot refinance or borrow in the future—and millions won't be able to for years—huge segments of our economy will continue to underperform or collapse. I propose that the weighing placed on 30-, 60-, 90-, and 120-day late marks on credit reports, bankruptcy, and foreclosures be diminished and not counted as heavily in the FICO score during this relief period. This alone would put major confidence back in the hands of struggling consumers and businesses. Anyone who was forced into foreclosure or bankruptcy during this time will have the black mark removed in three to five years, instead of ten years, so they can get back on their feet.

Many Americans and businesses will not have access to the market for credit or home loans in the future. And even now, with rates at all-time lows, it is irrelevant because so many people can't get loans to take advantage of the low rates. Those Americans who pay their bills but are falling behind should be given relief, and this is one way to do it very quickly. When it can take an individual months or years of struggle to remove one bad mark from their credit score, but it only takes one second for it to get there—even if it is not correct or not even theirs—it's time for the system to be overhauled.

Debt Consolidation

Here is another idea that doesn't require any government money. In fact, none of these ideas require the government to borrow more money to spend on the ridiculous and failed strategies that got us here.

Why not allow all Americans, rich and poor, to consolidate debt under one payment so the toxicity of the bank loans and credit portfolios isn't as bad? If we can use the government smartly to drive and backstop a program of debt consolidation—not bailout—everyone would be much better off, and in many cases better able to pay back what they owe. Those with bad credit would have constraints for several years on any additional credit or financing so they can get their present affairs under control. This also would help the imminent crisis that Freddie Mac and Fannie Mae are staring at. The government instead is minting and borrowing money to acquire all these loans and credits with cash, although some of it is necessary to make sure the large banks have liquidity and don't collapse. But doesn't it make more sense to proactively get all institutions to immediately help ALL Americans with debt to get it under control instead of just writing it off? Also, this would be a huge uplift for the mortgage industry, housing industry, banking industry, and others, as refinancing is a very lucrative business and will also free up consumer's disposable income. A program like this would help every single American, unlike the current foreclosure plan that very, very few can even qualify for. The paper that piece of legislation was written on belongs in the bathroom. If they can backstop Freddie and Fannie with $5 trillion, why on earth wouldn't they try to go to the root of the whole problem? Oh, did I again say that the government had to borrow any money from the world just to spend it?

Liberation Day

If we can quickly buy back our foreign debt, then we are in a tremendous position of strength, and ALL trade deals and interactions financially with the UN, World Bank, and other nations should immediately be brought under one non-political financial team. America has almost no leverage now with China and other nations as a result of the massive amounts of U.S. debt they own. With the debt owned by American institutions, we can renegotiate our position in the world aggressively. Sick the capitalist dogs on them, I say!

I believe that a Department of Homeland Financial Security, just like the Department of Homeland Security, needs to be formed. Career politicians, lawyers, lobbyists, and some other smart people occupy DC (along with many of the incompetent), but when it comes to economic war and managing a checkbook, I have no confidence in them. We are a capitalist nation, but our sovereignty has already been sold away, and our balance sheet and profit-and-loss statement look worse than a pink-sheet stock. We need a CEO, board of directors, and management team completely divorced from any political machine. Don't you think it's time to have some of our best and brightest overseeing and managing our national capitalistic affairs?

NO MORE LIPSTICK OR PERFUME ON THE WASHINGTON PIG!
Clean Up Washington with One Move—Have Civilians Manage or Oversee the Budget

Although lawmakers would fight this bitterly and would immediately hide behind the Constitution, we must recognize and conclude that we are going bankrupt as a nation and are likely already in a bankruptcy spiral for which the lawmakers are to blame. This certainly does not apply to *all* lawmakers, but whoever said lawmakers are qualified to be money managers and the businessmen and women who control our financial destiny? The Constitution clearly states that Congress has the authority over financial and budgetary matters and exclusively the power to appropriate funds and to borrow money on the credit of the United States. This is called the "Power of the Purse." Unequivocally it is Congress that has buried the United States under a mountain of debt, and it continues to make it far worse.

Almost everything our lawmakers do is tied to borrowing and spending money. Do you see many actual laws being drawn up that aren't full of pet projects and excessive spending? It appears Washington's only grasp on power is through the control of the money. I can't remember when I have seen a pure law passed that has been on television, can you?

Do you want DC cleaned up? Do you want our country to survive economic disaster and future downfall? Then we need to get our money out of the lawmakers' hands, or at a minimum have a civilian agency established to oversee every single penny, and not some rubber-stamp group. Without total control of the money, lobbyists, campaign donors, and special interests would lose all interest in what our lawmakers are doing, because they would not be able to influence the laws of the land, which heretofore often have been designed to directly benefit them financially.

Don't think this will ever fly? Well, how about a national referendum—a ballot item in every state and municipality across the country. This would apply to federal, state, and local spending. Eventually, it could become a constitutional amendment, which I think would be one of the most powerful in American history.

UP or DOWN Vote!

Up! I, as a U.S. citizen, want Congress, the Senate, and the White House to manage the federal budget and to be able to exclusively appropriate funds and to borrow money on the credit of the United States.

Down! I, as a U.S. citizen, want our best money managers and businesspeople to manage or substantially oversee the federal budget and the budgets of all state and local governments.

What do you think the outcome would be? I am not a pollster, but if you ask anyone on the street—anywhere in America—the resounding and overwhelming response would be to get the budget out of the hands of Congress or to create a substantial civilian group to oversee it.

Aside from the national debt and pork spending on issues like the Prairie Highway and turtle tunnels, people continue to reelect career politicians when many Americans can't eat or be properly educated in this country. We are allowing lawmakers to flush our country down the toilet and we do nothing about it.

MORE IDEAS

You want some more ideas about how to get us on the right track? Here are a few more.

Put Those Getting Unemployment Checks to Work

Using stimulus money and tax credits to get businesses to hire workers is simply backwards. This will not stimulate job growth when the businesses are hobbled and projecting a bleak scenario. You think they want to hire a bunch of people so they can write it off on their taxes? Who the heck thought of this one? Maybe some very big businesses can take advantage of it, but the vast majority of businesses need to fight to survive right now. Wouldn't it make sense to get the unemployed workers we pay anyway inserted into the work force while we pay for them? This would supply the market with many people who can do community service, work for businesses and even the government, while they receive benefits and still allot them the time to look for a new job. Who thought of hiring a work force of temporary employees for the Census when the unemployed could have done it? The answer to that is political gain through positive job numbers. Doesn't it just make sense to have the unemployed working at least part time to help dig us out of this mess? How many small businesses would benefit? How many large ones? I suspect when we start to see any glimmer of light at the end of the tunnel that many of the unemployed may be kept on at their government-funded jobs after unemployment runs out. That's when tax incentives should be used to reward businesses that have screened workers and worked with them for a while to retain them, not hire new. Frankly, the way the government wants to do it with the tax credits is just backwards.

Eliminate Capital Gains

So you invest wisely, take risk, and maybe make some money for your retirement, and the government gets 15 percent of your profit when you sell your investment? As if this wasn't egregious enough, there are some elected officials who are proposing to increase that percentage to 20 percent and much more. This tragedy appears to be imminent. Let's take a hatchet and cut off more of our fingers and toes!

Consider this scenario: I make $5 per share investing in Microsoft. I took a risk and supported Microsoft. I invested $75 total dollars and sold at $80 a share (making $1,200). A good return! Well, I forfeit almost $180 of my earnings—much more of it under the new tax laws—just for having done the right thing and assuming the risk to invest in our economy. The capital gains tax does more to stall and cheat our economy than almost any other thing. Putting a hold on the capital gains tax for several years or, even better, doing away with it would draw huge sums of money into the market, and stocks would have a massive surge. This most definitely would result in more money in the pockets of consumers and companies, who would then have an incentive to save, invest, and spend, shore up the emaciated retirement benefit plans we now know are broke, and help the portfolio of every American to recover their massive losses. I will cover more about the horrid U.S. tax system, which aside from making me sick, costs all of us and the government hundreds of billions, if not over a trillion, each year just to navigate it and hundreds of billions, if not over a trillion, hours of productivity.

Commercialize Education: Free-Market Public Education

We are now far behind many nations in educating our children. The most important asset we have in America is being nurtured in the most inadequate way. Everyone in DC is looking to spend hundreds of billions of dollars to upgrade and overhaul systems. But they are spending most of that money on computers, buildings, and infrastructure—not directly on the young minds we need to educate. This is why so many people turn to private education, but many others simply can't afford it.

Peel the wool from your eyes! Not everyone is getting an equal education. For a large percentage of the population, the education is completely inadequate. As long as this persists, our society will remain largely stratified—the rich maintain power and influence, and the poor and middle class stay where they are, not having access to the many opportunities that a high quality education could offer them.

Think of this! Our society rewards investment bankers, bond traders, and even scandalous CEOs with hundreds of millions of dollars. Teachers, law enforcement, military, firemen, and other professions vital to our lives are some of the most underpaid workers in the country. What does it say about society when the educators who are building our future, the first responders who are saving our lives, and our military personnel are often paid less than house cleaners, auto workers, and bank tellers! Government cannot and will not correct this problem effectively.

The only solution I can envision, and it doesn't cost the government one dollar, is to enhance our education system by commercializing public schools and finding inventive ways to clean up the system with for-profit means. For example: product branding for lunch meals, books, and sneakers—like a grocery store selling shelf space for products to be sold in their stores. The same type of revenue-generating space can be sold for products on school shelves. Marketing and ad revenue can be generated from many brands—for example, Microsoft,

Apple, Disney, or Nike—that target this demographic. All products and services would have to meet stringent guidelines for efficacy, children friendliness, and relevance and be perpetually held to the highest standards. I believe whatever it takes to create the revenue needed to revamp our schools and attract and pay the brightest and best teachers is necessary to change the massive downturn in our education system.

We all see that school districts across the nation are cutting way back and having to shut down schools. It is clear that the hoards of people overseeing education districts and even school finances are at best severely underqualified and fiscally inept. So how do we make sure new monies for education overhaul are spent appropriately and intelligently? The obvious thing is to pool the monies under each district and have for-profit managers, accountants, and fiscal experts manage it. With all the problems we hear daily on the news that states, municipalities, school districts, and our government face, why on earth do we continue to allow the same people who have broken the bank to be left in charge of fiscal matters.

Commercializing schools using products, advertising, and for-profit offerings is a clear way to raise huge sums of the much-needed money to change our failing system and external fiscal management is a necessary step. Under a program like this there are many opportunities to turn schools into for-profit ventures so the best teachers can be hired, and those who think "tenure not performance" is a worthy measure may just find themselves as a ghost with a résumé in a new free-market educational system.

Commercialize Government

Have you been to the unemployment office, department of motor vehicles, or any government-run office that provides services for marriage licenses, fish and game licenses, property tax, or anything related to state, local, and federal agencies where direct interaction with a worker is required? There is a high probability you walked out of there ready to pull your hair out because of the government's low level of customer service, minimalistic work effort, and the waste of hours and hours of your valuable time. Just to add salt to the wound, you actually pay for all those government agencies and all those workers.

If private companies were created to provide services like these, such headaches would never happen. Why? Because you would not frequent them! You would go down the street to a company with better and more streamlined services and those that are tailored to meet your needs. Competition would force each private company to provide the best, most efficient service and at the most fair prices. You are the customer, after all.

Why on earth does our government run large segments of our national administration? If Social Security, Medicare, and Medicaid were run privately or by public companies, and they managed the programs like the government does, it would be Enron to the power of ten.

The government could save hundreds of billions of dollars, and likely over a trillion dollars, annually by making sweeping commercial changes: reducing the size of government, enhancing profitability, eliminating all the fat and waste, securing the future of programs and systems for retirement and benefits, and offering better service, innovative programs, and new progressive solutions that address the market's needs. The savings alone to the government would be considerable. The infrastructure and expense offloaded to the private sector and the income to the government for the services under contract would remain a very large source of funds to perhaps, in our wildest dreams, replenish Social Security. Doesn't this make sense instead of growing an already-broken government with borrowed dollars? This is not just the federal government, but all those broke and broken state and municipal governments too.

Help for the Real Estate Industry: Money Grows on Trees

The United States and international real estate values have collapsed. Property owners are desperate to uncover any added value that can help sell their property and defend the asking price to salvage whatever equity they may have had in their property. Agents and owners are using every tool imaginable—360° views of the property, marketing brochures, Web sites, direct mail, television, and many other means—to help sell their properties and to present their valuation case. Did anyone realize that landscaping on a property is a considerable asset that grows over time, and in the case of a home is usually more valuable than an entire kitchen, electronics, and appliances combined? Granite counter tops, flooring, cabinets, and even the kitchen sink disposal are selling features of a home, but tens of thousands of dollars' worth of landscaping is only noted as "good curb appeal" and "nicely landscaped" on an appraisal. Essentially this means you dug a hole and put your money in the ground because it has no tangible value that can be measured.

To date, appraisers could never value landscaping assets on a property. Buyers and sellers could never asses the value or inspect its health when buying or selling a home. Hundreds of billions of dollars have been spent and tens of billions are spent annually on landscaping products, services, trees, and shrubs. So why wouldn't this asset be valued and used to help sell a property? Well, that's easy, nobody knows they can!

Seven years ago I cofounded (created) Horticultural Asset Management (HMI). We focused on the property casualty industry to value the replacement cost of landscaping assets for claims and property cleanup after storms and other events where landscaping was damaged or wiped out. There are over five thousand arborists and tree-care companies covering 75 percent of the U.S. population that go out to properties to appraise these assets for the company. HMI has become an industry standard valuation methodology for plants and trees, much like color, cut and clarity are used for diamonds. At that time I did not project a total collapse of the real estate market and the values of properties. But now I see the light. With that, I have been hard at work on another solution!

Go outside or on the drive home tonight, look at your landscaping and your neighbors'. I can assure you that if you have new landscaping or existing landscaping, it is way more valuable than you ever thought. For example, when a new tree or shrub is purchased, it triples in value when you place it in its setting: your yard. Anyone ever buy a diamond for say twelve thousand dollars and a ring for one thousand dollars. When the diamond is placed in the ring setting, the appraisal usually triples, if not more. Most of us have all been through this before.

So I have determined that appraising one's landscaping can be a considerable uplift to the real estate industry and will help you sell your property and defend the value of your home or commercial property. Heck, I would really want to know if the landscaping is healthy and won't die on me after I buy a property too. So we went right to work creating an actual book, based solely on your property and plants, as a marketing tool for Realtors or yourself. It provides color pictures of all your trees and shrubs, care instructions, a health score of the plants, what to do to make them healthy, and of course, the value of the plants and total landscaping. Fun for the whole family! Now I may be crazy, but when the market hit the wall, I immediately went to work on this. I am not sure if it will change the market-driven comparable value of a home, but I know for a fact that uncovering tens of thousands of dollars of landscaping on your property will help defend its value in a sale and may even provide an appraiser with a number that has never been available to them.

Give me a few months to maneuver, and then go to www.moneygrowsontrees.com and we will get an arborist to visit you and perform the service. This seems a logical way to help the real estate industry doesn't it?

2

An Economic Playbook 2010

The Economy May Be Bottoming Out, But Main Street Will Remain Under Water

Economists are being conservative in a quarter-by-quarter analysis of how and when the U.S. economy and housing market will recover. This analysis is based on manufacturing output, exports, new and existing home sales, and a host of variables. Everyone is watching GDP growth—especially when compared to last year. I am of the opinion that a lemonade stand would look positive against the last year. Expect that when "big business" begins to revive itself, it will take some time. Don't expect a big bounce, but rather slow growth, more pains than projected, and a gradual increase (if not stagnate) for some time. The key will be you and me getting back to buying products, goods, and services. Consumption has always been the key. Without it, no economy can survive.

The unemployed and underemployed are a huge factor in recovery because they are nervous, scared, and broke. These consumers are more than likely to have curbed their spending habits already and will be unable to consume as they once did for some time. Instead, they will focus on rebuilding their lives—that is, if they can ever get a job. Expect this to further impact domestic growth. It was credit spending that artificially boosted the economy for so long. Now, the credit addicted can't get credit, and the credit worthy aren't going to spend enough to make it up.

It is logical to state a fact that the heart of recovery is consumption, but even with home sales spiking in some areas, real estate consumption is still stagnant and decimated in many areas. High-priced homes aren't selling, and many people can't qualify for loans anyway, especially not for larger homes (this shoe is dropping quickly too). Owners are watching their equity dwindle as homes sit on the market for long periods of time. Even if they sell their home, most people are eating up their equity just to get rid of it. So even if the housing numbers are up or even way up, know that the sellers are selling at a loss. This just adds more fuel to the fire, because they get even less money to spend or to buy another home. The real estate market will continue to pose a problem, and even more shoes will drop for certain.

As you can see, I am sour on the recovery, however modest it will be. The psychology of Americans may be temporarily boosted by public relations campaigns about consumer spending, but under that veneer, Joe the Plumber is still hurting, and so is the global economy. Expect chest pounding about all of the great things our government is doing to "stimulate" the economy, but remember that any so-called boosts in retail and other sectors are the result of big businesses offering discounted services and blow-out sales of inventory just to restock their shelves with more stuff people can't or won't buy. Although it looks good on paper and allows for more political entertainment and advertising, the fact is that they are still making less money although sales are up! You sell something for five dollars one day, and you blow it out for two dollars the next—well, there goes your profit. In other words, this is not a recipe for sustainable recovery. You and I both know that toward election time every glimmer of hope in the jobs market—any straw to be grasped—anything at all they think can be shoved down our throats will be pandered and sold with any and every talking point they can come up with. If you are going to buy any of this and not remember, come election time, then you deserve to be led by the nose and have your head stuffed in a toilet so you can swallow more of what they are selling to you.

3

How Did the Financial Collapse Happen?

NOW LET'S GET DOWN to understanding how America, the financial industry, politics, and the economy have gone so wrong. Let us start with the financial industry and what happened. This is the simplified version.

Confidence was lost in the U.S. housing and credit markets and the securities that banks, insurance companies, and investment banks used to support it. When you or I get a mortgage, the banks do not keep that loan on their books. Sure, they lend you the money, but then they take thousands of mortgages just like ours and bundle them into various financial vehicles, some you may recognize, for example, CMO (collateralized mortgage obligation), CDO (collateralized debt obligation), or ABS (asset-backed securities). For decades this process had been used by banks, mortgage companies, and Wall Street to securitize the mortgages, sell all the paper to the bond market, and make huge amounts of money while doing so.

By securitizing (securing the bond being sold by the underlying assets and the cash flow from people paying on the mortgages or on other credit types), the banks can loan money at one rate and then sell the mortgages and other credit types at a lower rate to get more money and do it all over again.

Here is an example that will help you to understand my point: I have a $300,000 mortgage at 10 percent interest. You have a $300,000 mortgage at 10 percent interest. The bank lends out a total of $600,000 to me and you. Then the bank takes thousands of similar loans, bundles them, and sells them to the bond market. In this example, the bank gets back the $600,000 it loaned you and me by selling our mortgages, and now it can lend the $600,000 again. The trick is that banks, insurance companies, and investment banks use credit-enhancement techniques to insure against or to buffer potential losses. Credit enhancement is a kind of backstop that can absorb potential losses from defaults on the underlying loans in a pool of collateral (mortgages, credit card receivables, etc.). There are many techniques that would complicate this explanation (as if it were not already complicated), such as overcollateralization, wraps, or buying credit default swaps (derivatives) to take a 10 percent loan bundle (my mortgage and yours in this case) and insure its credit worthiness. By insuring the performance of those mortgages—buffering or offsetting potential bad asset performance—the risk of loan bundling is reduced. The bank would recoup its $600,000 at a lower rate than the original 10 percent interest. So what should have been a BBB-rated, BB-rated, and many even lower portfolio of mortgages and other credit types became, with credit enhancement, A-, AA-, and AAA-rated portfolios. The cost of borrowing for all the banks went from a high percentage to a very low percentage because the underlying credit no longer looked as risky as it really was. Now the banks could get liquidity at a low interest rate and re-lend the money at higher rates, therefore making money on loans. This case is even worse in the subprime market.

It sounds complicated, and it really is, but this has been going on for many decades, and banks have it down to an actuarial science. The financial institutions know within a few percentage points what a portfolio of one thousand 10-percent mortgages will pay out. You and I may pay our mortgages to maturity; others may refinance at five, ten, or fifteen years; some borrowers will default; and some homes will burn down. Statistically the cash flows of the mortgages are nailed down to the penny, and such confidence allowed all of this to occur. Sound familiar? What happens if confidence is lost in U.S.-guaranteed investments like T-Bills and bonds? Right at the beginning of the meltdown, I said that banks, investment banks, insurance companies, and reinsurance companies would get caught with their proverbial pants down—and they did. What happened, and this relates to our national deficit and debt too, was that the financial markets lost confidence in the U.S. housing market and other related financial instruments. This may have resulted from plummeting housing values or simply predicting that bankruptcies and defaults, for instance, would erode the future cash flows from mortgage owners or credit card holders and the CDOs themselves, and therefore, the underlying assets bundled in the CDOs were no longer considered creditworthy. What happened next is the key, however. The liquidity and ability to sell and refinance these portfolios dried up in a very short period of time. A multi-trillion-dollar marketplace just stopped. The banks and investment banks were left holding huge numbers of mortgages that they wanted to bundle and sell, and they owned and had issued many CDOs and all types of credit enhancement and hedge investments themselves. But the liquidity for the mortgages, credit enhancement, and other products was no longer accessible, and they couldn't unload them. Without that cash coming back to them, the financial institutions were left without a means to get more money to shore up their coffers. Worse, many of them were on the hook to cover losses in the portfolios themselves. This problem turned out to be as bad or worse—and not yet over—because, through the various products, backdrops, buffers, and insurance, they have to pay up when the piper came calling—and he did! This is one the major underpinnings of the worst financial crisis since the Great Depression.

4

Einstein Was Right About the Financial Industry Meltdown

> Two things are infinite: the universe and human stupidity; and I'm not sure about the universe.
>
> —*Albert Einstein*

WHAT CAUSED THE FINANCIAL industry meltdown: greed or stupidity? Take a look at the definition of stupidity: willful ignorance or unintelligence. This quality can be related to a person's actions, words, or beliefs or those of a group.

This meltdown should drive every American to riot! The massive loss of money, homes, livelihoods, and economic credibility are just the beginning. Who would have thought that America would just teeter up to another Great Depression, and Russia and China may be our Mr. Potter of *It's a Wonderful American Life*? And we are definitely not yet out of the woods by a long shot.

It doesn't take a fancy education or a financial expert to understand that Enron and WorldCom pale in comparison to the political and economic mismanagement of the leaders—business and political—who caused this debacle. It's the same fraud, greed, mismanagement, lying, and cheating that business executives have been jailed for. Executive decisions at every level were made that overleveraged banking reserves, rolled over mortgage portfolios and other credit types by borrowing from the financial markets through collateralized debt obligations, and had to borrow billions to stay afloat. Sound familiar? Yes, this is just like what the United States does at the treasury auctions, only it has just happened to our financial institutions.

Is America Next?

Many of the pundits and media personalities now agree with me that the United States is bankrupt and heading for disaster. I have been blue in the face about it an also focused on the rating agencies, like the recent Moody's alarm sounding that are getting close to downgrading the U.S. debt like what has happened in Greece and potentially other European countries. And I assure you this will happen if we get close to $20 trillion in debt!

The government, FDIC, and the Federal Reserve (the Fed) have stepped into our capitalist system, and this is only the tip of the iceberg. The American people and many around the world have lost over $1 trillion of real cash and wealth as a result of the market plummeting. Heck, these days you might get shot in urban America for a pair of sneakers. What do you do with the people who stood by and made hundreds of millions for letting this happen? The punishment for these people is loss of a job, millions of dollars for a golden parachute, a slap on the wrist, and a shoulder shrug. "Whoops!"

My opinion is that leaders, employees, and anyone at any level responsible for this meltdown and within individual institutions should all be standing before a judge. Everyone is claiming ignorance, hiding losses, and ducking responsibility.

If that wasn't bad enough, the Fed and FDIC had to step in to post bail for them and the companies they ran into the ground. Now the rest of the world is flush with money and is buying America's heart and soul.

You want to control capitalists and America? Wage economic war! Devastate our culture and way of life! Just wait for the system to collapse and buy it all up. Do you actually believe the Fed and FDIC can shore up our present collapse and the long line of banks and institutions and entire industries going under? Throw in the $5 trillion commitment to Freddie and Fannie. Do you believe we aren't over an economic barrel because of the actions within the ranks of banks, investment banks, traders, and the government? Do you actually believe the worst is behind us?

Think again!

And think hard about this. If the United States were a company, wouldn't our leaders all be fired and many in jail for the way they have run things.

> We are living on borrowed time and time is a luxury we just don't have any more. We can't solve problems by using the same kind of thinking we used when we created them.
>
> —*Albert Einstein*

5

How Greed Defines America

Greed is all right by the way, I think greed is healthy. You can be greedy and still feel good about yourself.
—*Ivan Boesky, disgraced and jailed financier*

GREED MAKES PEOPLE WANT to do things since they will be rewarded for their efforts. America is built on this principal, and it creates **enormous** wealth, opportunity, and innovation. But it is also one of the primary causes of the disintegration of our economy and society. Theft, fraud, abuse of power, reckless behavior, risk taking, pride, power, and politics are driven by greed. Advancement in our society, not just in the financial sector, is driven by personal desires to obtain a higher social status and the acquisition of wealth, power, and property. This beast is within us all, and very few tame it. And now the genie is out of the bottle.

In the case of large financial institutions and companies that have failed, are failing, or have caused catastrophic economic conditions, the greed behind the fall is excessive and appalling at best. We have all heard about the contractual obligations that had to be paid with government money to some of the very traders and leaders who sank the ship. Where are the moral obligations of these people? The fact is this: there is little correlation between morality and greed.

Sure, in good times derivatives traders, investment bankers, and heads of corporations can make billions in bonuses. Yes, billions, not just hundreds of millions when you add it all up. Executives and employees who reap enormous rewards for running their businesses and our money into the ground are the very ones who are profiting. Regular Joes like you and me certainly aren't profiting! This is the way the financial industry and the business world works. People get paid when they generate gains, but they do not give back when their actions cause havoc and massive economic loss. So how do we navigate this issue that has Americans screaming in anger and disbelief?

Some executives forfeited their bonuses and reduced their salaries. That was a start. You would think that everyone involved in a company's collapse would forgo being paid bonuses for the actions that caused the collapse. AIG is the highest-profile company to pay out bonuses after the collapse to employees who had contracts. Why can't we use the Securities and Exchange Commission to change the laws and protect against this ridiculous behavior? This wouldn't be unprecedented. In 2002 the SEC implemented the Sarbanes Oxley laws, also known as the Public Company Accounting Reform and Investor Protection Act of 2002. This legislation came as a response to a number of major corporate and accounting scandals, such as Enron, Tyco International, Adelphia, and WorldCom. Well, the current economic meltdown is much more damning than those illegal scams. But instead, we just sit back and allow it happen.

Outrage isn't enough! The bonuses were paid across the board even for the most grossly negligent and inferior executives in the world. The first thing shareholders and the government should do is stop signing any contracts with public companies that have golden parachutes, guaranteed bonuses, and contract buyout clauses. If you botch it as an executive and get the boot, why should the shareholders pay you? Of course, on the flip side, if the executives perform well, then, and only then, should they reap any rewards. This would use greed in a positive way as people would be incentivized to act within the rule of law and drive the businesses they run in the right direction in order not to lose their income or have to repay some of the money they received.

As I am finishing updating this book with current examples, Congress is trying to pass sweeping financial reform legislation, just like HealthCaid, as quickly as it can before the midterm elections. This will happen, and it will happen too quickly for anyone to dig out the implications buried in the bill. Everyone wants blood and political equity, but I fear that rushing this legislation through will create only more problems and only more bureaucracy.

We have to be very careful how this is done. People are fearful that placing huge oversight and constraints on our financial sector will stifle the industry, the stock market, and the investment we so desperately need from these groups to keep the economy going. Sweeping policy changes and oversight will only create more government, and I assure you that many domestic and international companies will quickly stop doing their business here, or at a minimum, move a great deal of their operations overseas. Passing financial reform legislation (which I agree is much needed) so quickly for political gain has horrifying consequences. Just horrifying. We need to make sure we do this absolutely right!

6

The *Titanic*

Is the U.S. Economy and Big Business Too Big to Sink? Too big to fail! We have heard this repeatedly, and the headlines these days are ripe with political posturing and pandering for votes by holding a gun to the head of our capitalist system. Throughout history, we read the same label about the great ocean liner *Titanic*. Industry after industry keeps running aground as the government continues to bail water out of sinking ships. How do we save the ship when the lifeboats have all been used? What's next? Pensions? Hedge funds? Retailers? Airlines? How can the United States keep printing and borrowing money to plug the leaks and stay afloat? *It can't!* If you bail out the water and replace it with the burden of debt and huge amounts of new currency, you will sink for sure.

The collapse of the U.S. economy is upon us, and polls show that many of us for the first time in our history are worried that this will happen in our lifetime. The ship hit a mortgage iceberg first, then insurance, and the hull keeps ripping at every turn. George W. Bush was right to call Wall Street "drunk," but I would throw in the politicians too. Remember the *Exxon Valdez*. Like that ship's captain, the people steering our economic ship were drunk too. Even now, they are so hungover, their heads are not screwed on right. While the government believes in bailing out companies that are too big to fail—such as GM and the country's largest banks—we all sit around on the second- and third-class decks, powerless to do anything but drown. The iconic bread lines that came to represent an individual's plight during the Great Depression are today filled by companies and entire industries waiting for a government handout. Everyone is looking to get a handout or bailout. But government is not the answer.

During the 1980s, 1990s, and early 2000s, the companies we see trying to get a place in today's bread line had aggregated (bought up) so many businesses that they became too big to fail. So the government has to bail them out? At this point in history the answer is yes, because our whole economy would have collapsed otherwise. But why hasn't someone thought of a plan to break up these businesses? For example, GM's finance division would be a huge IPO and would reap billions for GM, its shareholders, and the private equity investors who own a large portion of the business. GE Finance and Chrysler Credit Corporation are other examples, and the same goes for banks and insurance companies. The leveraged buyout funds are just licking their lips, ready to begin buying assets from failed businesses and turning them around. Why isn't the government forcing the issue?

If you take government money, the government should force a de-bundling of car brands, insurance lines, and bank brokerages. If the government lends the money, it can recover the capital quickly through the sale of assets and IPOs, which will regenerate the markets and streamline big business. Just look at AIG's success now in selling business lines for billions. Now doesn't that sound more plausible? I am so relieved to see some businesses doing this in earnest while being guided by new, strong leadership, like AIG.

Can the U.S. Economy Be Sustained this Way?

It can't. But the government's choice is to print money 24/7. Isn't it clear that this strategy will devalue the dollar and put our currency at risk? I believe the government's plans for economic stimulus are flawed. The bailouts are too, even if we take large ownership stakes in businesses to reassure the shareholders—you and me—that the money being invested is repaid. But if we bail out the airline industry or the auto industry, then what happens when people can't buy a car or afford to travel? The auto industry will be set to fail again. The government is trying to play it smart by casting off lifeboats. But the government is at the helm, and I am certain the policies being implemented will sink the ship. And remember, you and I are trapped on the ship too. Well, grab a life jacket and prepare to jump into some freezing water. You and I are sure to economically die either way.

7

Wall Street and K Street

Not Just Drunk...Alcoholics

Years of Out-of-Control Borrowing and Spending Shake Up Our Way of Life

Together Wall Street and K Street should be thrown into rehab. Their hand-slapping version of justice is like a night in a drunk tank. If America were a company, we would be insolvent. Our foreign debt holders would have already taken over the business, and there would be a long line of people going to jail. Our financial, political, and corporate leaders engaged in unacceptable behavior that has caused the worse peril to our way of life since the Great Depression. The midterm elections better do more than just shake things up.

Can America's greatest depression be avoided? Are lawmakers and business leaders willing to dramatically change America? I think every American would respond, "Absolutely not." If they were surveyed, a huge majority would respond with absolute outrage at how our country's finances have been squandered and our economy mismanaged to the brink of catastrophe. Many public-opinion polls are showing this now, and the Tea Party is growing as a national movement while many try everything to denigrate the movement—even lowering themselves to using the race card. Thank God all that is backfiring and just fueling more contempt for the politicians and attracting tens of thousands of people to join in the dissent!

Although the American people didn't run up the national debt or cause the dollar to be jeopardized, the American people are having to prop up mortgage giants Fannie and Freddie, giant banks, and insurance companies, and they are feeling a pain that's only going to get worse. The meltdown of insurance and reinsurance giants, hedge funds, pension plans, and retirement plans, the runaway deficit, the soon-to-melt dollar, the numerous bank collapses, and a myriad of things to come will cascade through the economy far beyond the financial industry and will affect every business around the world. Like a tsunami caused by an underground earthquake that shakes the earth, the real devastation is not felt until the huge waves follow. Our economy hasn't felt the full force of the meltdown yet!

Americans need to understand how and why this has happened, and moreover, they need to find a way out of the mess. I do not foresee any politicians coming up with a plan, other than new taxes (even with the help of the esteemed Debt Committee that was recently established). Mark my words, if something of biblical proportions isn't done to change our country's direction, the three-hundred-year-plus experiment in capitalism will end very badly!

America's Drunk Drivers Finally Wrecked the Car

Politicians and the Fed Hit a Huge Wall (Street)

Lehman Brothers, Washington Mutual, Wachovia, Merrill Lynch, and other sacred American financial institutions went bankrupt or had to be bailed out and sold at mere pennies on the dollar. Freddie and Fannie have little hope of being saved in the long run, even as the Fed mints money to save them. Oh, don't forget that government has committed trillions of dollars to backstop them! I don't see that or the tens of trillions of dollars in other liabilities and guarantees on the balance sheet the government uses to stick under our noses. America is applying bandages on issues and avoiding the radical treatment necessary to save our economy. What are our leaders doing and why are they doing it? At this grave time, are they playing politics as usual?

Lies and accusations are being tossed around the emergency room, along with the putrid mud we see during every election cycle. The car wreck has already happened, and the American body is traumatized. Where are the surgeons and the statesmen who can fix this? I don't see or hear anything that makes me believe politicians actually grasp what's going on. The Fed has to keep wheeling the crash cart in just to keep the heart beating, but that's not going to keep us alive for long.

Instead, the auto, airline, energy, financial services, and retail industries are getting pounded, and we are allowing foreign governments to take over. Someone somewhere needs to do something, and not just simple triage and a few stitches. This is open-heart surgery and brain trauma!

I say brain trauma because we must have lost our minds to let our economy continue to melt down. And our politicians keep shoveling the same garbage down our throats every day. We are hooked up to lifelines from across the world, and our government hopes everything will be okay if it guarantees more and more debt. Well, it won't be.

Even States Bellying Up: How About IOUs!

The economies of some of America's largest states are in jeopardy of bankruptcy and collapse. Who would have ever thought that we would see such chaos and fiscal mismanagement across the nation? It is hard to believe that California, one of the world's largest economies, is on the brink of bankruptcy. Just wait for the long line of states facing the same or worse problems. It is not just the federal government; it is an epidemic among state and local governments too—we just don't hear much about them. Is this the writing on the wall for the federal government? You bet! This should be taken with the utmost seriousness on Capitol Hill—or should I say Capitol *Cliff*? Because that is what America is teetering on while our government has the pedal to the floor.

Does anyone see the borrowing and spending coming to a halt at the state or federal level? I have read that 86 percent of a polling sample have no confidence in our government. When state governments across the nation are in dire need of money and facing political stalemate after stalemate, what is their answer? More borrowing! California is issuing IOUs to keep itself afloat! That means more debt on top of mountains of debt. Our currency and treasuries are not dissimilar—these are IOUs to the world. How long can the states and the federal government keep the house of cards from collapsing?

This house of cards is cracking from the inside and from the outside. We are fighting a multiple-front war against collapse—like the Wizard of Oz pulling all the levers behind a curtain of promises—and pandering social programs that are further bankrupting America. Do we have any way of changing this? Poll the people again, and I bet an overwhelming majority would say no! Write a letter to your congressman? I tried to send some of my ideas to my representative and senator. If they won't listen to me on innovative solutions like the 10 percent solution to buy back our national debt, why would they listen to you? The only reason would be if you could be publicized and exploited all over television for some political gain. I suspect this book will be right in the strike zone for movements like the Tea Party, and I hope so. It may be just the venue to get some good ideas from me and others out there on a national stage.

Even if the states get their act together and steer clear of a political, social, or financial meltdown, what changes would they make to end the irresponsibility? None! Things won't change until we run off Capitol Cliff. Change in our nation is reactive, not proactive. The world is looking, and when it sees states like California teetering on the brink of bankruptcy, what do you think this says about America herself?

8

Department of Homeland Financial Security

The American CEO

If you want a real solution to the crisis in DC and our country, don't elect someone to do it. Hire them! We need an American CEO, an American board of directors, and a fiscal management team that cannot be elected to the office but can be fired at any moment, just like the business world. The CEO and his staff would oversee the budget, investments, trade deals, currency hoarding and printing, and all fiscal parts of our government, even some in concert with the Federal Reserve. We have set up a Department of Homeland Security, why not create a Department of Homeland Financial Security? We are, after all, a capitalist country, and economic war and chaos are looming.

Pork, special interest, waste, and abuse have been running rampant in Washington for so many years that we are desensitized to it. Our nation needs financial managers—not lawyers and career politicians—to oversee our money. Worse, foreign nations, individuals, and corporations contribute to election campaigns in order to unduly influence Washington and expect favors in return for their contributions. This is at the heart of the problem. Do you believe we can clean it up if the budget was managed outside of Congress or, at least, under considerable civilian oversight? Take away the ability to borrow and spend our money irresponsibly, and see how fast the special interests lose interest!

9

America Is a Consumption Economy

The Economy Cannot Recover Without Consumer Spending

I am bewildered that our government leaders often fail to recognize the simple fact that America is a consumption economy. Yes, we make things and innovate, but the foundation of this country is Americans buying products, goods, and services. If Americans can't or won't consume, then the simple truth is that every sector of the economy will be devastated until that is corrected.

Here is a simple scenario. Bail out the auto industry. Who is going to buy a new car? Very few! So wouldn't simple logic indicate that the automakers would find themselves going right back to the trough again, because they still can't sell cars? Absolutely! Clunker or no clunker. Herein is the logic for every industry: if the consumers don't come back to the table (and unfortunately millions just can't because the effect of the downturn on their lives), then there will be no sustained economic turnaround.

Do we really think people are going to be traveling all over the world? No! They can't afford to. Add to that the credit card companies that are cutting up to 40 percent of the available credit to consumers, as they have been doing over the past twenty-four months. Go ahead and pay your bill, but your credit limit will be reduced going forward to the amount your debt has been reduced to each time you pay. The consumer is already cut off from home equity, refinancing options, and credit. Well, what does that do to the consumption economy businesses depend on? It wrecks it further and longer. Even better, start raising taxes—especially on the very people we need to spend and invest more money—yes, those who make over $250,000 a year!

I used the car wreck analogy previously because businesses like the auto industry are bailed out even if you and I don't agree with the decision, and consumers will not or cannot buy cars. Consumers are unemployed. Even with another "Great Works" program, consumers supporting the economy will find themselves underemployed compared to their incomes and benefits before the crash. Will the fifty thousand people let go by Citibank or those from Microsoft start building roads? How would you like to see the investment bankers, mortgage brokers, bond traders, and high-paid employees mixing concrete, waving red flags on the side of the road, and digging holes? You know that will never happen. These types of programs may be temporarily good for job numbers and political equity, but overall it will fail to correct the massive waves of chaos that have hit our shores and will continue to drown many industry sectors until consumers can resume consuming.

Everyone is culpable in this massive upheaval—consumers, banks, credit card companies—but that is yesterday. Remember this: no matter where go, there you are! So here we are, watching the corpses of consumers rotting on the credit and consumption battlefield while big business and big government run right over them. Mark my words: a stimulus package—with pandered money, tax breaks for more than 80 percent of Americans, tax credits for hiring workers, huge government programs to help employment figures (like the Census temporary workers), etc. is an appalling waste of money.

10

Unemployable and Underemployment

THE NUMBER OF JOBLESS Americans now exceeds the figures from 1967 and continues to approach historic levels. In California, unemployment has already reached a historic high. But *unemployable* and *underemployment* are the words we need to understand. Rising taxes, universal HealthCaid, unemployment extensions, more government, and a host of other programs ensures that unemployment continues. Another bleak fact is that many workers face a worse reality: they are unemployable. As terrifying as that is for families, it is a stark reality. Even if the workers in ghost towns created by business and plant closings—and this is not just in the auto industry that we hear so much about—could get a job, they would be underemployed at best. What options do they have? What work may be available for them in their ghost town? Barber? Walmart greeter? Street cleaner? If an industry leaves a town, there is nothing left for the former employees. If these people live in large cities, they will never see the kind of wages they were earning prior to being laid off, forced into retirement, or losing their jobs. These figures are as important to our economy as unemployment is. Workers who make less simply spend less. Period!

The unemployment figures issued by the government are up and down week to week. Political machines look for anything they can turn into political theater. But the reality is that unemployment numbers will continue to rise so long as industries such as defense, retail, and finance continue to get hammered *and* see their taxes go up *and* have to take huge write downs for HealthCaid (for AT&T that amount is one billion dollars). Across the economy we see write downs like this. What do you think the companies could do with that money? Hire some people? Right! The fact that fewer companies may be laying off fewer workers has little bearing on the fact that many workers who find work are very *underemployed.* Did you see all the chest thumping about how many jobs were saved by the stimulus? Where did they come up with those figures? Isn't it reprehensible that they would stoop so low to sell a rosy picture.

What is going to happen when the auto sector is hobbled again, now that the clunker program is finished? What will all those towns and workers do? We focus on manufacturing output, but up and down the supply chains, auto dealerships, retail shops, parts and clothing manufacturers, vehicle and home finance, and others will still have layoffs and bankruptcy. This hasn't yet ended. We see the unemployment figures rise and fall, but they are not the only useful numbers in portraying our economic strength. In fact, the U.S. consumption economy will lose so much more participation from the underemployed—those whose incomes are far less than what they were earning before the crash—a classification forgotten, overlooked, and devastating to families and our economy.

Find me some economists who factor those astounding numbers into the economic forecast, consumer confidence, and overall jobs picture in our country. Even better, hike everyone's taxes and make America close to number one in the world for corporate taxation and for sure more companies will jump off the sinking ship and build overseas leaving American workers behind.

11

Americans Go to Rehab

A Nation Addicted to Credit Is Forced to Go Cold Turkey

Most American consumers use debt to buy goods, houses, cars, and even groceries these days. These consumers are the foundation of our economy, and the ripples of credit withdrawal haven't been reported or factored into the meltdown. Banks desperate to survive the credit and liquidity crunch are cutting off access to credit, and their risk management groups are closing bank accounts and freezing or reducing credit card limits, and lines of credit. You didn't have to be a psychic to predict what happened during Christmas 2008, the beginning of the spiral for retail. And now that Christmas 2009 is behind us, here we go again, selling all this positive news when we know sales were driven by sales at blowout prices.

Cold turkey! America must realize that credit rehab is upon us. Cars, appliances, travel, food, recreation, clothes, and so on cannot be purchased if Americans don't have any money or access to money. The squeeze is on, and everyone is tightening his or her belt these days. Every business will feel the banking crisis, and the banks trying to survive will be at the root of a further economic freefall. The banks' credit tightening brings the problem right to our doorstep and will force millions of consumers and businesses out of the buying game that keeps America's fragile economy afloat.

The Consumer Confidence Index, based on polling five thousand households, is an important number to the Fed and Wall Street that gauges the relative financial health, spending power, and confidence of the average consumer. Consumer Confidence fell eleven points in the February 2010 poll to 46 percent. Do you realize how bad that is? Worse is that it rose slightly in March, and the horns start blowing, promoting how good that is. It's a crock. An even better indicator is to watch as sales of products, goods, and services in America dwindle and rise and dwindle again while buying power shrinks and credit is maxed. You are going to see a lot of store brands going under—many already have, and the majority have already closed stores all over the country just to survive. Retail sales figures go up and down each month, with some of the worst months in history just over our shoulder. In fact, American consumers have refinanced, borrowed, and leveraged their future with credit. When it runs out or the piper comes calling, what do you think will happen? Boom! Bankruptcy, credit counseling, and 30-, 60-, 90-, and 120-day late payments, which then only exacerbate the problem.

There is no credit methadone to ease the withdrawal. As a nation, we have spent, borrowed, and sold ourselves into bondage. The sucking sound you hear isn't just money, it is the lifeblood of our nation, our economy, and its consumers.

12

Economic Prozac

How to Avoid Another Great Depression

I was asked to present some of my thoughts on the nationally syndicated *Steve Malzberg Show* in New York in August 2008. Rita Cosby was the host, and Ross Perot appeared as a guest just before me. The economic crisis, political pandering, and empty promises topped the list of topics that day. America has been teetering on the brink of another Great Depression while politicians and political parties pander for votes from the largely undereducated voters in America. In August 2008, the *Washington Post* released a story about the economy and compared the Great Depression indicators to where we are today. America is being eaten up by a cancer while our society is further disintegrating, and the political parties offer nothing more than some Prozac to cover up the looming idea of a depression and are now calling it "the Great Recession." Isn't it convenient they coin all these terms to make it easier for us to swallow?

America is facing one of the most challenging and potentially devastating crises in our short history. Despite the facts, politicians and their parties keep stuffing the talking points du jour down our throats with hundreds of millions of dollars being spent to make sure we swallow it and don't choke on the garbage. America is in big trouble, and as usual, I predict we will wait until the devastation occurs again instead of going on a massive offensive. This nation needs to mobilize every tool in the shed as if World War III—an economic war—was upon us. Frankly, it is. We can all point a finger, lay blame, and talk from the armchair. It's time to realize this: you are either making it happen, watching it happen, or letting it happen to you! And I assure you, it is happening to us.

There is no easy cure for a debtor nation's woes, but, worse, no one is prescribing a solution to the looming problems that can destroy our way of life. It sounds harsh, but what will America look like after the fall of Rome? Where will our ego and standing in the world wind up? And when is the proverbial piper going to come for our currency and debt.

To me, the national debt is outright insanity. This has made us vulnerable to major nations that could cut off our credit, just like so many banks are doing to their customers. Our nation is now a risky investment, and our currency is losing its footing as the underpinning of world trade. And still our government keeps borrowing and borrowing and borrowing to survive.

The economic disaster isn't going away. We haven't seen the other shoe drop yet, but it will, I can assure you. Just look at the headlines about Social Security going into the red much earlier than all those smart politicians and government economists have predicted. I've been ranting since the financial meltdown occurred that the initial $300 billion written off by banks was a small part of the total amount of bad debt on their books. I went on radio across the country and asked, "Where is the other $700 billion of bad debts that haven't been accounted for?" Well, we found out, didn't we? An additional, massive $700 billion bailout! Before it is all over, this will be more than a $2 trillion for the bailout and stimulus plan.

The bailout came in after the train wreck and was supposed to clean this up? Enough is enough. We treated Wall

Street with antidepressants, and we've given them to the world too, so they will be happy with America and support the markets. The hiking of the FDIC insurance on bank accounts to $250,000 is economic Prozac and a very low dose at that. It is meant to stabilize and reduce consumers' fears so they don't make a run on the banks to withdraw their money. If investors and consumers are not well emotionally, selloffs and a myriad of other consequences will be upon us. Just check out what happened when the lawmakers didn't pass the financial bailout initially: one of the worst stock market declines in history.

13

Oliver Twist

Please, Sir, Can I Have More Money from the Government?

There's a run on the federal government by many giant companies just like the union-hobbled airlines or Amtrack have done in the past. Big companies are running to the government for help—again! How many times is the airline industry, for example, going to get in line as it has done time and time again? The auto, finance, and airline industries are just a few of the many mouths to feed. This has been going on for decades, but it has become far worse recently. Like little Oliver Twist asking for more meat, please. When do the handouts stop?

The bailout of the auto industry is being followed by a growing line of companies seeking government handouts. And what we don't see is the U.S. balance-sheet money being used to help industries and government-backed institutions suffering from the effects of a long-term cancer. If we were using accounting the right way, all the liabilities the United States is on the hook for—not just the borrowing of money, but contingent liabilities (liabilities that the government or a company has committed to but not funded presently, which may come due in the future)—would be apparent. Then you would realize the tens of trillions of dollars our government company is exposed to in addition to the more than $100 trillion we simply need down the road for all the government and social programs.

If you want to be appalled, go to www.usdebtclock.org. Be sure to wear a bib, because the numbers will make you sick.

The government is wrapping itself and feeble businesses and industries with so many bandages that they look like mummies. But mummies are already dead when they are wrapped up, and I'm afraid this is going to be the case for many companies, industries, and our nation.

There are many capitalist plans that could be implemented, and if we don't pursue them or force them to happen, this economic crash will just be the fuel that spreads the cancer we already have little hope of recovering from. With or without our input, these bailouts have and will continue to happen. And the companies lining up will not stop until the federal government puts its foot on the necks of the failing industries and gets out of the commercial lending arena.

14

Pandering for Money from China

The United States Is Begging to Borrow More Money

Timothy Geithner made an unprecedented trip to China last year to reassure the Chinese authorities that the United States remains a good investment. He was following up on a visit by Secretary of State Hillary Clinton, who urged China to keep buying U.S. debt. Thus the United States apparently goes hat in hand to make sure it can continue to borrow money from the Chinese to spend on bailouts, big government, and assorted failed polices. The government is borrowing trillions of dollars so it can make loans and investments on our behalf. That is called buying stock and debt on margin, and it is the fundamental issue that caused the 1929 stock market crash that led to the Great Depression.

The world is losing confidence in the United States' ability to support its borrowing and spending habits and its treasury instruments and currency. This couldn't be more evident than by the need to ask our Chinese benefactors for more money. In fact, some people in the audience at Geithner's speech in China laughed at him for saying the full faith and trust of the U.S. government is behind our debt and currency. It is the same as the Oliver Twist scenario I painted earlier. Even our government is standing in line to beg for money from China in exchange for IOUs.

If we don't continue to borrow money from the world, the federal government and the U.S. economy will come to a screeching halt. I can't imagine that the world will continue to allow the United States to borrow and spend for everything our administration and future administrations ask for. Our debt is coming home to roost *now,* and I believe our entire culture is in jeopardy.

Think about this. We would need tens of trillions of dollars in the bank today to fund programs like Social Security and many more into the future. Where did the original money in the Social Security account go? Years ago lawmakers passed a law that allowed them to trade IOUs for the money in the fund. You see, the out-of-control spending by our government has a long history. Now, every time you pay the Social Security tax out of your paycheck, that money goes to pay for other programs and entitlements—*not* just Social Security—and they use government instruments backed by the "full faith" of the government to back them up. In fact, programs like Social Security own a huge percentage of our national debt. Taking money from the systems we all pay into, and then turn around and borrow from it to spend on other programs, earmarks, and pork is outrageous. Robbing Peter to pay Paul and constantly rolling over new money to replace old is what landed Bernie Madoff and others in jail—right? Expanding government and investing money for you and me in failed companies and systems has forced us all into a corner, and we have no say about how the government is bankrupting itself and us. Just look at HealthCaid.

The financial bailout was necessary to avoid the collapse of our financial markets. As horrible as it was, the scenario could have been much, much worse, and we are far from out of the woods. But when is enough enough? How we got ourselves into this catastrophe doesn't matter anymore. What does matter is how we will ever get ourselves out of it in our lifetime. Frankly, I don't see any way the United States can avoid being cut off from the world, and I see no policies or behaviors in DC that will stop that from happening. The banks were cut off from rolling over debt, but the government continues to do the same thing. We will get caught the same way. It is just a matter of time. If we cannot keep borrowing from the rest of the world and giving IOUs to programs like Social Security, what do you think is going to happen? Do you think the stock market will remain stable? Do you really think our government can continue to operate? Unless radical and aggressive plans are enacted immediately, this country, our industries, and our way of life will be driven into the ground. In fact, we are already sitting in an economic coffin just waiting to be buried.

15

The Wizard of Oz

Pulling Strings from Behind the Curtain

DON'T WE ALL WISH we could wake up from this nightmare? The problem is that there are no ruby slippers, and this isn't the American dream. Our children are born in debt with a plastic spoon in their mouths. When will the world look behind the curtain and see that the United States is a house of cards? Worse I am positive they already have and are likely sick over it.

I wonder if our Founding Fathers would have envisioned trillions of dollars of debt and much more coming and the minting of trillions of dollars of new money. They must be rolling over in their graves. Here is a quote from Thomas Jefferson—it's quite profound:

> I sincerely believe...that banking establishments are more dangerous than standing armies, and that the principle of spending money to be paid by posterity under the name of funding is but swindling futurity on a large scale.

Sound familiar? How can we continue to survive as a capitalist nation if we are gambling everything on future prosperity? Whoops! Wasn't that a big part of the rationale Congress relied on to sell us HealthCaid. They said it would save billions and would be offset and even pay for itself from future economic growth. Projecting that any program, especially a government program, will save money and pay for itself is like throwing rocks at the sun. I can get better odds in Vegas. This program will not pay for itself and we all know it! Mark my words: HealthCaid will demand trillions of dollars we don't have for another social welfare and handout system we can't afford. And it will require hundreds of billions of dollars annually to support as it moves forward.

History will show that the time the United States began its decline was when we shifted away from the gold standard. There are so many quotes from ages ago around this issue that I got tired of reading them. It is a crystal ball into our future. It's not roosters we should be wary of; it's the foxes that have already ate them all.

So it appears the solution is to spend, borrow, and print money like there is no tomorrow, and frankly, there isn't. Not only has our economy taken a one-two-three punch, but we are betting our future on ourselves to win. How can we possibly play Russian roulette and not think the bullet is going to hit us? The mighty Wizard of Oz was feared and adored, but he turned out to be a weak old man behind a curtain. In our case, with the American dollar flooding the market, treasury auctions, and debt skyrocketing, we won't be as lucky if the curtain is pulled back.

16

The Economy

An Unnatural Disaster

America Faces Its Biggest National Security Crisis—The Economy

LIONS AND TIGERS AND Bear Stearns—OH, MY! Fannie and Freddie, Indy Bank, Countrywide, Lehman Brothers, Merrill Lynch, Washington Mutual, and many more to come. And wait! That's not all! The fire sale of America is happening. What other skeletons are hiding in our economy's closet? A lot more than you read about, for certain! Propping up our nation's financial institutions and industries is like putting a piece of bubble gum scraped from your shoe on a leaking dam.

It's not the beginning of the end for everyone, but it's the beginning of the end for a lot of financial institutions, investors, and many others. What if all the money the Fed is printing day and night comes back to haunt us. And, worse, what if we are attacked and another trillion dollars is ripped from our economy like after 9/11?

It's not just the private sector and banks; it's the rest of the world's people, countries, and institutions that are losing hundreds of billions of dollars. The mortgage meltdown and related crises is America's face to the world presently. The world's confidence in America is stretched so thin that just one more straw may break the camel's back—or U.S. bank.

Any nation on earth right now could topple America. For

instance, if China or Russia want to pull the plug, it would be much worse than the mortgage meltdown. The U.S. economy has become one of our biggest national security crises. Even the CIA agrees. I believe it is by far the gravest. Our nation is predicated on the foundation of our economic strength, but our economic strength is collapsing around us while the world is watching. What if a terrorist event happened? BANG! A two-by-four right to the head! And if our enemies wanted to crush us further, they could simply adjust investments, lending, or buying...although, heck, they already own us anyway. What if foreign nations decided to sell off some of the treasuries they own, like Japan almost did back in the 1990s when their system collapsed. Yes, it would lead to a run on the bank!

The government cannot shore up the failing economy and credit system piecemeal. America needs to take unilateral and massive action on many fronts to stave off an economic disaster that will leave us vulnerable to the whims of the world's nations. But this is already happening. Dubai and Greece are prime examples of what is coming. I just hope the glue keeping it all together holds up.

The National Debt: A National Security Crisis

> While we play checkers, the Chinese and Russians play chess.
>
> —*David Oppenheimer, sitting in my study*

On September 11, 2001, we all watched in horror as planes struck the World Trade Center and the Pentagon and crashed in a Pennsylvania field. I was on a plane to Denver that day. We underestimated the resolve and intellect of our enemy. They struck us then, and they will again. We think they live in caves and howl at the moon...and many do. However, the specter that lies behind these groups in the shadows and in the international corridors of power knows of a much easier way to take down America—our economy.

Our recourse after 9/11, militaristically speaking, was absolutely one-sided. America pummeled two cultures, and we were hand in hand in unity across the nation and in Congress. We responded massively, but that kind of action won't save us now, because our leaders won't act with the same courage, resolve, and unity when it comes to the economy.

After 9/11, the U.S. economy lost over one trillion dollars of value along with three thousand lives, a hole in the Pentagon, and the destruction of the World Trade Center. That was tragic, but it is nothing compared to the devastation the United States caused in Afghanistan, Iraq, and around the world. Believe it or not, the enemy is sophisticated and more than aware that the U.S. system is based on confidence, which any debtor nation must maintain in order to keep its head above water and continue to attract foreign governments to buy and own our debt and currency. Do you think our enemies know this to be absolutely true? You had better believe they do, and they know we are being held captive by the world. Do we think Osama Bin Laden is our only enemy? Not all of our enemies wear a uniform or carry a gun.

I wonder if we all recognize our own Achilles heel.

ECONOMIC WARFARE

The United States is dependent on China, Russia, and the rest of the world. Oil dependency pales in comparison to America's dependence on having foreign countries buy our debt. The attacks of 9/11 ripped one trillion dollars of value out of our financial markets. The losses incurred by Freddie and

Fannie, IndyMac, AIG, Bear Stearns, Lehman Brothers, Washington Mutual, and many more are much worse. The real reason the Fed and FICA rushed in to shore up the nation's institutions is our dependency on our *credit worthiness* in the eyes of the world. If America loses its footing and the world nations stop propping up our government by constantly buying our debt, America will plunge off a cliff. If China or Russia wanted to topple our way of life, they don't have to use military force. America's vulnerability is our economy.

America is playing checkers while the world is playing chess. With China, for example, which owns hundreds of billions of U.S. debt and trillions of dollars of our currency, we are over a barrel and completely dependent on their faith in our financial system. How can we ever play hardball with these nations? In fact, China uses its leverage as a "nuclear option" if the United States plays too hard in trade deals.

Ever see the scene in *It's a Wonderful Life* where everyone makes a run on the Bailey Brothers Building and Loan? Check out IndyMac, Wachovia, and Washington Mutual. People were walking out of those banks with their savings like their predecessors did during the Great Depression. We thought people making a $16.7 billion nine-day run on the banks like Washington Mutual were a thing of the past. But it's happening again right here in America! A few more pushes, a few more collapses, and the house of cards will fall down.

17

Nationalizing Banks, Auto, and Insurance

The Government Is Our New Stockbroker

The U.S. Taxpayer's New Portfolio of Stocks

We the people have a new stockbroker: the U.S. government. On our behalf, the government has a discretionary account. This means, as a broker, the government has the discretion to invest and lend without our input. So what are we investing in?

Let's start with one trillion dollars in our brokerage account as an example. The government is lending and has already loaned most of that money to various companies, banks, brokerages, automobile companies, and insurance companies. This is equivalent to having a secured interest in these companies with the hope that the loans will be paid back, much like when the bank uses your home as a secured interest against a loan. The government has tried to take into account the risk of the loans by charging a very high interest rate. The higher interest rates are to be expected because these investments are the equivalent of buying junk bonds. So our portfolio is growing with very high-risk assets, almost like a venture capital or venture lending company would undertake.

In addition, the government is taking large equity stakes

and what are called warrants to further risk-adjust our investments. Warrants allow the government to buy stock in the future at a set price, typically very low, and when the stock rises, it makes money on the difference between the strike price (the negotiated set price) and the stock price when the stock is bought and sold. Actually this occurs as a cashless exchange, because the government pays a fee to buy and sell the stock simultaneously and nets the profits for our portfolio.

Further, our broker is buying stock or receiving stock in the companies for making loans or for purchasing shares of the businesses held in treasury so the companies can unload stock not already floating in the public market and take the proceeds directly into their businesses. This is the case with CitiGroup. This, too, is at a negotiated price, typically below market value. This creates what is called a market overhang. A simple way to put it is that the shares now held in our portfolio have been purchased below market value, and the market knows this. Knowing the stock is owned at this price and there is a guarantee of selling the stock when the price goes up shapes what the street value of the stock is. Often, because the amount of shares owned is so large, the value typically goes below or hovers around the price the government paid for it. The government recently publicized it intention to unload its CitiGroup position, and if you have watched the stock, it has trickled up and down, hovering around the government's purchase price. As the government sells off its position, we could actually make some money to offset other losses sure to come.

So what does this mean for our investments? We now hold and are accumulating very risky assets and high-interest loans. This combination is exactly how the venture capital industry works. The way money is made by a venture capital group is that many of the investments and loans fail, perhaps even eight out of ten. Some venture capitalists do better than others. The idea is that the two successful investments are so successful that the entire portfolio of investments is paid back and a substantial profit is made. For example, if we invest $100 million in ten private companies, say $10 million each, we might lose $80 million on the eight dogs. But we also invested early in Cisco and Apple computers, and we make an astronomical amount of profit from the successes of those two companies. Will this be the case in the portfolio the government has created for us? Not very likely!

Here is the bottom line. Our new portfolio grows as every loan and investment—like the TARP program, bank loans, and the bailout of GM—is made. The risk we are taking is so high, the expected returns should be commensurate with the risk. But they won't be. Hopefully the way our government is investing our money, we can at least get back our money, but that is unlikely. Even more remote is that we make a profit.

This is the reality of what our broker is doing on our behalf. Do I think our money is safe? No. Not by a long shot. Do I think we will get back at least our original investment? Maybe some of it, and in our wildest dreams, we may even make a profit. The jury is out on our broker's ability to execute that feat. Let us all pray they are good enough to perform.

18

GM = Government Motors

THE GOVERNMENT CALLS IT SACRIFICE—I CALL IT BEING WIPED OUT

WIPED OUT! All of your GM stock—whether you are a private citizen, an institutional investor, an auto worker, or anyone else who held stock in GM—was lost last year. I watched the president's news conference where he called on shareholders to make a "sacrifice." *Sacrifice!* This was not a sacrifice. It was a complete loss of your investment. But we have to sit still and eat it!

Much worse was that the unions ended up getting a huge stake in the business, despite their being a major part of the problem in many industries, not just auto manufacturing. If you don't think that was buying future votes, then get your eyes examined. We are not investing in these companies; we are borrowing money from the world to loan this money. So we shore up the balance sheets of all of these companies while our own balance sheet is so upside down, we are essentially getting a bailout from the rest of the world. Do you think Clinton's and Geithner's going to China was a coincidence?

Fiat swooped in on Chrysler. A surgical bankruptcy? Some of GM's assets were sold to Germany. The government took over 60 percent of GM. Come on! Who is buying cars? Can you afford to run out and get a new car? Trading in clunkers was an artificial lift to the industry. But that program was over almost before it began. And GM lost billions again! Will consumers buy so-called green cars that will eventually be built in America? Creating the capacity to produce them here will require a massive investment by our auto industry, it will take years and years, and the auto makers are already broke. Will they accept a tax credit (fueled by borrowed money) to trade in their cars for a more fuel-efficient car? Or will consumers shift heavily into foreign cars and buy even more than they already do? In fact, if consumers want green cars, they will buy foreign products because foreign car makers are way ahead of U.S. manufacturers in fuel efficiency and hybrid technology. The problem with U.S. automakers (among many others) is that the industry is just broken. Throwing money at it won't repair it at all.

A Solution for the Auto Industry

This will be short and to the point. Like the 10 percent solution to buy back and retire our national debt, I have another radical idea. (Didn't the government say it wants radical ideas and change?)

If I were bailing out the auto industry, I would create a new company. Let's call it Auto Manufacturing USA. Each automaker would contribute its manufacturing capacity—plant, property, equipment, and union contracts—to the new company. The new company then would look across all plants, product lines, and capabilities and streamline the production of automobiles for the sector and even foreign manufacturing. The optimization of the auto manufacturing sector—the challenge and massive investment required to convert the plants and cars to being more green and updating antiquated operations—could be addressed under one business strategy. The best operations would be kept, others upgraded, and all the plants retooled with the ability to produce one another's cars. And those toxic unions could be brought under control so they don't keep sinking the ships they are riding on!

The automakers would liberate huge assets on their balance sheet. Liabilities and operating capital to run those operations would be shed. I am certain the potential IPO or massive private equity investments for the new company would create a windfall of capital for the auto industry and provide the capital the new company would need to upgrade, phase out, and retool the manufacturing lines and create new ways to produce cars. Liberating all those assets and moving the expense of those major operations and work force would free automakers to do what they do as well as any company in the world: research and development, product marketing and distribution, finance, and automotive innovation. Another radical idea is for competitors in other struggling industries to team up to make these types of ideas a reality so that American manufacturing has a fighting chance on the world stage. Wouldn't this also make sense to consider this type of plan for their stakeholders? Do you think this a good way to get America caught up with the rest of the world and to become more competitive again? Wouldn't this claw back some of America's manufacturing edge so we can actually get back to making things here again?

19

What the Numbers Mean to Main Street

World Bank, Unemployment, Trillions in Spending

Is there an end in sight? Nope! The news keeps getting worse, and the projections made by our government should not surprise us when they are hundreds of billions of dollars off. But what do all these facts and figures mean to us?

Unemployment

Unemployment exceeding 10 percent in modern America is a catastrophe and equivalent to an American nightmare come true. The figures, as vile as they are, do not represent all the facts. If the underemployed and unemployable were added, we would have a more accurate picture, and believe me, it is far worse than 10 percent. The picture state by state is even worse. This also means that a large portion of workers in America are being wiped out. In order to pay bills, people are raiding their savings, stocks, mutual funds, and 401(k)s every day. Are these numbers reported? No! Americans are just given the broad strokes.

Contraction of Growth

The World Bank is right when it reports that the world has become an economically smaller place. Some people may take solace in this fact, but a vast majority don't. But as the world goes, so does the United States and vice versa. If the world can't consume, then the writing is on the wall. Yes, more layoffs and unemployment and more businesses failing because they can't sell products, goods, and services. Look at the airline industry's solution: raise rates and charge extra for baggage and make it even more unaffordable to travel for those who don't have the money. Last night I spent almost twenty dollars for three roast beef sandwiches and some fries at a fast-food franchise. So raise prices to make up for losses in other areas? Car dealers, construction, you name it. At least Walmart is hanging in there, but that's another story.

Currency

The presses are running day and night. A lot of people think there is a gold-laden Fort Knox somewhere. Well, there isn't. Currency is just paper, and the United States isn't the only nation printing it. The tragic thing is that currency is not backed up by anything except the world's faith in governments. This means the more currency that's out there, the more commoditized it becomes. And that means inflation is coming, and it's coming hard! Inflation will devastate already hobbled consumers. Americans are just broke, and there are millions who are broken. When history writes about the fall of America, the abandonment of the gold standard will be recorded as one of the most detrimental decisions ever made.

Spending, HealthCaid, and Welfare

Spending isn't quite accurate. We are borrowing to spend. HealthCaid reform for one trillion dollars? Our government is crazy! We can't afford the debt we already have, and we want to borrow more for screwed-up entitlement programs that have already been pilfered! Federal programs like Medicare, Medicaid, and Social Security own a huge portion of the U.S. debt. Where is the money? What happened to tort reform? Well, the lawyers' lobbyists are obviously not to be fooled with. Therefore, insurance premiums for doctors are so astronomical that, combined with taxes, many physicians can't keep their heads afloat. So create a huge government entity and fuel it with borrowed money. Meanwhile, the people who provide services have nothing but insurance nightmares. Sickening!

Stimulus

The G8 nations have concluded that it needs to stop. Why? They can't afford it. Well the American government already pandered this to us, and instead of retracting all their spending and unrealistic promises, they put trillions of debt on our debt to follow through on things that are not possible to achieve without further bankrupting the nation. Now take into account the tens if not hundreds of billions of dollars that have been spent on pork-barrel projects that politicians can claim credit for in their communities in order to be reelected. Is this working? Absolutely not! There are way too many pigs at the trough to ever see the money pour onto Main Street. These people couldn't even pass a stimulus bill without earmarks and backroom political payoffs, and HealthCaid's backroom deals are absolutely appalling.

We see the headlines and political entertainment geared to pull the wool over our eyes. Wouldn't you agree that 90 percent or more of what we see our lawmakers actually do is borrow to spend money?

We are told we must think of "our children and grandchildren" and that we must "leave this a better place then we found it." Well, forget about that. It is *us* we should be worried about, because in our lifetime we may see America's collapse.

20

Marxism vs. Capitalism vs. Socialism and Redistribution of Wealth

The Communist Manifesto

If you turn to chapter 2 of *The Communist Manifesto,* written in 1848 by Karl Marx and Friedrich Engels, you will find the first five principles of communism:

1. Abolition of property in land and application of all rents of land to public purposes.
2. A heavy progressive or graduated income tax.
3. Abolition of all rights of inheritance.
4. Confiscation of the property of all emigrants and rebels.
5. Centralization of credit in the hands of the state, by means of a national bank with State capital and an exclusive monopoly.

The top three principles are of particular interest today!

1. Take control of and redistribute assets.
2. Impose a heavy progressive or graduated income tax.
3. Abolish all rights of inheritance.

Marx and Engels presented a total of ten measures, and the progressive, highly punitive income tax has influenced tax systems around the world. Their goal of economic justice is wide ranging, but an underpinning element of their philosophy is that the masses will be reliant for their subsistence on wealth redistributed by the state. Sound familiar? Just these first three principles have been or are being introduced widely in the United States. Did I hear "redistribution of wealth" in the last election? Although I don't think our leaders are communists, our system of taxation certainly approaches this philosophy. A redistribution of wealth to support the other 50 percent of the country that doesn't pay any taxes is insane. If our government leaders are truly focused on redistributing wealth (as they have clearly stated), then we are taking a page right out of this playbook.

The Capitalist Manifesto

Written by Louis O. Kelso and Mortimer J. Adler, the underpinning of this philosophy is the concentration of capital. While it may undermine a free and democratic order, a higher order of economic justice is that everyone has a human right and an equal opportunity to become an owner of capital. Isn't this supposed to be the American Dream? Philosophers dating as far back as Aristotle have contested that property is essential to preserving a free society. So you want to seize my capital property (this includes cash by the way) and give it to others by means of unfair and discriminatory taxes biased toward one class of citizen over another class? This is not capitalism!

Socialism

At its core, socialism is an economic system governed by a political elite who hold concentrated ownership of production and wield more economic power than they would in a capitalist system. This system is characterized by big government and out-of-control spending (and borrowing to do so). Politicians have complete discretion regarding expenditures (with no public oversight), and they are not constrained by the will of the people, because our voices just don't matter. Power rests solely in the hands of this political bourgeois. As our federal government becomes bigger and increasingly pervasive, this nation becomes more socialist. Given the laws enacted in 2009 and early 2010, our country seems to me to be moving toward socialism.

The Web site of the Center for Economic and Social Justice highlights the differences between a capitalist and a socialist political system. I advise you to visit http://www.cesj.org/thirdway/comparison3rdway.htm. You will be thrown for a loop when you read the socialist column.

21

Financial Discrimination

Should the Government Be Sued?

If you make over $250,000 a year, you will be the victim of discrimination under laws being contemplated in Washington. Taxing me differently than others in our society, treating me and others as a different class of citizen, and touting class warfare is, not only unfair, but it is either unconstitutional, discriminatory, illegal, or all the above. This argument has legal standing if we just follow the laws already enacted by the very lawmakers who now want to single out a class of citizens to redistribute wealth disproportionately. This is as fundamental an argument as the ERA, civil rights, discrimination laws, and others that have been made at the state and federal level. Treating citizens differently, applying the law to them differently, and profiling them based on financial status are obvious violations of our rights. This is a fundamental argument that should be the basis for tax reform and having a flat tax system by adding taxes to products, goods, and services instead of income so everyone is treated equally as a means of generating revenue to run the country. This is what states like Florida, Texas, and Tennessee do, and see how well they are doing!

Developed countries—not just the United States—mandate that people must be dealt with on an equal basis, regardless of sex, race, ethnicity, nationality, sexuality, and religious or political views. This applies to employment, consumer transactions, and political participation. The horrifying thing is that a capitalist nation would discriminate against its most successful citizens—roughly 5 percent of the population is proclaimed to be affluent—most of whom employ many of the other 95 percent. For example, taking mortgage interest deductions away from only the $250,000-and-above earners and raising various taxes only on them is the very definition of discrimination. And heretofore laws have been passed to protect the victims of discrimination. These actions are just wrong, but there is an extensive legal, moral, and civil history directly based on discrimination of one class by another.

GENETIC DISCRIMINATION VS. BEHAVIORAL DISCRIMINATION

In short, anti-discrimination law refers to people's right to be treated equally. Genetic discrimination—which is discrimination based on race, sex, and disability—is illegal. Behavioral discrimination, however, is not considered illegal.

In a capitalist nation, it is my *behavior* that has resulted in my making more than $250,000 a year. Therefore, financial discrimination is not necessarily illegal. What recourse, then, do I have? I would have to modify my behavior to make less money in order to not be discriminated against. That's *insane!*

For working hard, achieving, and being successful, I am singled out, as are the others in this 5-percent category, and labeled, stigmatized, and segregated from the overwhelming majority of citizens. This group is now being targeted by proposed and new laws that apply only to them and not the other 95 percent. This is clearly a discriminatory practice because it is a delineation of one segment or group from another for the purpose of treating that group differently. Worse, this stigmatism and segregation has been publicly lauded, and the government is the very body that says it, believes it, and is discriminating against a class of citizen forced into this category.

I mentioned behavioral discrimination as not being illegal, but I protest! There are many behaviors protected by state and federal law and our Constitution. Gay rights, gay marriage, and abortion, for example. And here is a whopper: religion. These are all behavioral choices. You choose to live a gay lifestyle. You choose what religion you wish to practice. You choose to abort and kill an unborn child. So these groups are free to behave the way they want, and businesses, the government, and others cannot discriminate against them and have to treat them equally. In fact, their rights are defended with billions of dollars annually and have caused some of the most controversial debates in America.

So why is my behavior to make money in America not protected from discrimination? Where is the ACLU in all this? When are the lawyers going to line up to protect my rights! It doesn't matter if you are rich or poor; this is just outright wrong!

22

HealthCaid Makes Me Sick

I AM JUST SICK over this—we cannot afford the major HealthCaid reform the president and Congress just passed! These reforms were stuffed down our throats and will cause many insured taxpayers to actually pay more for these services as another form of welfare. Also, for the first time in history, American's are being forced by their government to buy a product and take on a specific financial responsibility. I will say for the record the reform will be sued against as being unconstitutional—and yes it is already. Furthermore, Congress is using healthcare reform as just another opportunity to cut backroom deals and spend extra money on pork projects. The notorious Louisiana Purchase and the Cornhusker Kickback are perfect examples, and just look at all the recent backpedaling on both of them. We all know that in order to get the votes needed to pass legislation, deals are made—almost exclusively using borrowed money. So not only can we not afford this bill, but politicians are looking to extort ridiculous sums of money for their communities, just as they have done with the stimulus bill and so many other bills. If anyone actually dissected the healthcare bill—highlighting the massive amounts of money being allocated to each member of the Senate and House for their community projects—we would revolt!

A huge portion of the cost of care in America is liability

insurance. Someone cuts their finger in an office, and they sue for hundreds of thousands of dollars. A hot cup of coffee spills on someone's lap and a massive lawsuit is filed. So is it HealthCaid reform or is it tort reform that is necessary? Simply put, establishing another already broken system like Social Security, Medicare, and Medicaid (which is what this reform is doing) is not the answer. And leaving tort reform out of the bill is just wrong!

We are broke! There is a very real possibility that Americans won't have healthcare or a retirement pension coming from the U.S. government at all. The only proposal, and almost always the case, is to borrow and then spend more than a trillion dollars to "fix it" when the government has already spent a large amount of money in exchange for IOUs in other social welfare systems. I don't think so. If you think this program is only going to cost one trillion dollars, then you are dead wrong—it is beyond the Planet of the Apes to think so.

I suggest we immediately create a Medical Corps similar to the Peace Corps so that Americans can have access to an all-volunteer army of doctors trained to take care of the underprivileged. This would replace the flock of doctors and nurses who are going to walk out the door as a result of national healthcare. Why shouldn't our nation take many programs like the International Red Cross and the Peace Corps and refocus those resources to serve our citizens? Also, like the GI bill that supplements the savings of military personnel in order to afford college tuition, an MI bill would help pay for a doctor's education in exchange for a four-year commitment to serve the uninsured, and this would be part of their qualifying residency program. I assure you that HealthCaid will cause doctors to flee the industry and create a gaping hole in the infrastructure that is already strained to serve people today. In the interim, all U.S.-based military healthcare personnel, VA hospitals, government-run facilities, and military base hospitals should be made available immediately for Americans to receive healthcare. If we don't augment healthcare facilities and care providers, the millions of newly insured Americans will cause the system to collapse under this weight. We already pay for all these facilities and care providers, so let's use them as much as we possibly can.

Consider this idea. The drug companies operating in the United States get a tax break and a donation tax credit to offer large supplies of drugs to the marketplace for the current entitlement programs. That is a huge chunk of expense for those who need it most. Instead, proposals on the table will tax this industry to death. The elderly already can't or can barely afford life-saving prescription drugs now, so this would be a huge relief for millions. Now take $475 billion out of Medicare to pay for HealthCaid and watch the enduing disaster. A big relief would be the amount of money the Medicare and Medicaid systems have to spend (whoops—borrow to spend!) to support drugs for all their constituents. This is a huge expense for these systems and can be dealt with intelligently instead of throwing money at it. Come November every mature citizen in the United States should walk, hobble, or get wheeled into the voting booth.

Here is a very personal example. My wife had a kidney stone while she was pregnant in Florida. She had to call 911 because I was in New York City. I rushed back. The hospital in Clearwater, Florida, treated her badly. It was the worst healthcare experience we have ever had. They even gave her a drug screening without consent, and believe me, she doesn't even drink—and neither do I. To add insult to injury, our insurance received a whopping bill for almost ten thousand dollars. Four hours of care and some tests cost ten thousand dollars! That is more than the cost of childbirth, which my wife and I found out on January 18 this year. What is wrong with this picture? If we move in the direction of socialized medicine, you better expect more of the same: inferior care, an exodus of high-quality doctors and nurses, overworked staffs, and horrifying experiences. If you want subpar care, then another welfare system is just for you.

Some Great Healthcare Solutions and Ideas

I would like to offer other ideas to resolve this healthcare reform issue.

Having healthcare for every American is something we should strive for, but at what cost? Massive cost. Overhauling the systems of care in the country—making us more like Canada, France, and Cuba—is so unwieldy that the system itself may be torn apart. We have the best healthcare in the world because we have a free-market medical system. In fact, many people from all over the world come here to receive the best care.

Using pooled insurance programs that are for-profit is a good way to spread the risk among a large universe of people. The insurance industry says that in order to make medical insurance more affordable, everyone needs to be a part of it. Statistically, increasing the population in the pool would result in insurance benefit payouts that will allow insurance program managers to invest the money collected and make money on the premiums, therefore making massive payouts for benefits affordable. That is how insurance companies operate. It's a capitalist system, and it works for insurance companies just as well as it does for Wall Street. Getting everyone into that statistical pool is the crux of the matter and mandating participation is just wrong. Having the federal government in this business and forcing people into its program is a disaster. Just watch and see! If you want younger, more healthy people in to spread the risk across the pool, then don't just use the healthcare bill to take over student loans (why this was in the bill is beyond me), but use the program to pull them into the system. If a student wants a loan in order to attend college, then require him or her to have health insurance as well, even if it means tacking it on to the borrowed money. This would be a huge population addition to the pool, and it would help the insurance industry to participate in the plan.

Despite this debacle, the main issue in healthcare today is the cost of care. Pharmaceutical giants make billions peddling their drugs and supplying them to every class of citizen, from babies to the elderly. Insurance companies make billions in the liability premiums paid by doctors, who are the very people trying to save your life. Now you want to levy huge taxes against the pharmaceutical and medical device industries. What do you think will happen? Right! The costs of their products and services will go up and be passed along to consumers.

Here are few more reasonable suggestions.

1. We can donate billions to solve AIDS in Africa, but what about using that money for AIDS in America? We spend so much around the world to promote and offer care, why shouldn't we redirect it to those Americans who need it badly? We can help take care of the rest of the world, but we can't take care of our own?

2. If you are receiving government benefits via welfare, Medicaid, or Medicare, you should have to perform civic duties to rebuild America. Focus as many of these citizens into the medical industry or other projects to better our society. We

need a huge addition of people into the healthcare system to handle everyone, and it would be a great education program for people who will learn new skills and have opportunities to be employed within the medical industry in the future.

3. Enact tort reform. Liability insurance is the greatest barrier to affordable access to quality care. Cut a finger in the doctor's office and someone will sue for millions. Although the lawyer's lobbyists will spend hundreds of millions of dollars to thwart this effort—and they are large contributors to both political parties—this one issue is a major cancer in the healthcare economy. The price of healthcare services has to rise to absorb the cost of these premiums, and this adds billions of dollars to the cost of care. So the very people who are saving your life are the very people being driven out of the industry and sued for trying to do so.

4. Encourage faith-based healthcare programs. How many thousands of trips and millions of people are taken by church groups annually to foreign nations to provide medical care? Why don't we incentivize the religious community to redirect those resources and the massive volunteer work force back here at home? Offer additional tax incentives for donors to fund the church organizations, and you will see a massive work force pitch in.

23

Trust in Our Lawmakers, the Federal Reserve, and Business Leaders

THE DEFINITION OF TRUST is a firm reliance on the integrity, ability, or character of a person or thing.

Andrew Jackson spoke these words in 1832 to a delegation of bankers.

> Gentlemen, I have had men watching you for a long time, and I am convinced that you have used the funds of the bank to speculate in the breadstuffs of the country. When you won, you divided the profits amongst you, and when you lost, you charged it to the bank. You tell me that if I take the deposits from the bank and annul its charter, I shall ruin ten thousand families. That may be true, gentlemen, but that is your sin! Should I let you go on, you will ruin fifty thousand families, and that would be my sin! You are a den of vipers and thieves. I intend to rout you out, and by the eternal God, I will rout you out.

A friend sent me that quote in 2008. I feel like a Paul Revere racing around the country trying to make a difference. I know you do too. Confidence and trust in our institutions, Congress, local politicians, and America has expired.

Do Americans and does the world trust America anymore? I can't remember how many times I have alerted the media about the erosion of world confidence in America and the dangers that would cause our nation. Even with this looming over us, Congress has not even passed a constitutional amendment that requires a balanced budget each year, which almost all the states have. Can you believe that? The self-regulated lawmakers have a great piece of critical legislation just sitting there in DC. This is one of the most important constitutional amendments in American history. Do you remember the last time we had a balanced budget? The national debt has grown every year since 1957. Now, with our debt at $13 trillion, how could our leaders let this happen? It's no wonder no one trusts our government.

Okay, now let's look at the definition of confidence: *Trust or faith in a person or thing.*

Horrifying isn't it! And we say America is a democracy. If America were truly a democracy, then we would be empowered to do something. But Americans feel impotent, unimportant, and hopeless. In actuality we elect representatives modeled on that of ancient Rome and empower, trust, and hold confidence in them. Read those definitions again just to make sure we are all on the same page.

How many Americans believe DC is acting fiscally responsible and always with our best interests in mind? I will bet my life and net worth that most Americans will say they are appalled, disgusted, and outraged. Why, then, if we have lost trust and confidence in this system, do we allow these people to run our country and institutions? Unfortunately, the American republic is an oligarchy: rule by the few, the rich, and the powerful. You are either in the club or not, so sit back and let them run your lives and country.

Imagine if in your home, workplace, or community no one trusted you or had confidence in your abilities. You would be fired and alienated by everyone around you. If you made broken promise after broken promise, what would the outcome be? Again, horrifying for you! And here we sit glued to the markets and our televisions just to be programmed and pandered to. It is hardly conceivable that we can take back our country. And as sad as it sounds, it is very likely the United States may have to declare bankruptcy in my lifetime, unless massive changes are made. The outcome will be the flushing of the dreams of millions down the toilet.

24

Elections

Giving Your Opinion

> If they want your opinion, they are happy to spend billions to give it to you.
>
> —*Billy G.*

THE MEDIA IS THE most powerful weapon of the twenty-first century. In fact, our election process has become a consumer branding process. What politicians do during campaigns is really no different from what Walmart, Proctor and Gamble, and Coke do when they advertise. In the 2008 presidential election, like most campaigns, the Obama team spent a large portion of its six hundred million dollars on advertising and outreach to voters. This does not include special interest and other groups putting ads on television. That is about how much is spent on developing a consumer brand over a period of time. As with other candidates, in Obama's case it was spent in just over one year. Face it! The American voter is ignorant and uneducated when it comes to elections, the economy, and international affairs. Informed decisions are almost impossible to make, and so the political machines will spend whatever it takes to give you your opinion.

I wish the ballot had a box of Tide on it to vote for. I trust that brand. Hundreds of millions of dollars have been spent to develop that brand—and guess what—it cleans things up! Now I would vote for that brand. Wouldn't you?

Billions are spent by politicians across the country at every level: local, state, and federal. Why would they spend any money if it didn't influence your opinion to vote for them? What if a candidate for CEO of a company made promises, denigrated his opponent, placed negative ads around the company, started false rumors, and used company money to execute a large portion of it? What if even more private money were raised from their friends in the company just to further their own ambitions? Worse, what if after they were hired they created pet projects, pork projects, and earmarked spending for the divisions and the people who got them elected just so they could turn around later and be reelected to their job? Do you think this behavior would get them hired? Even if they were somehow hired, do you think they would hold that job for long? Of course not! They would be fired, unemployable, and I would say without a doubt in jail.

With billions of dollars raised from private sources to support political campaigns, it is clear someone owes someone. Then the money is spent mostly on television advertising to influence the masses and "get out the vote." The leadership of our country at all levels is for sale. We all know elected politicians fight for money to be borrowed and then spent for their communities. Why? To benefit their constituents and communities and get reelected, of course! Having made all these promises just to get elected, the promises are then pushed and lobbied for with the hope they will get funded while all the others pile on their pet projects.

I don't think "We the people" will ever be able to stop or change the machine. There is way too much money to be made. Just think of how much money the media companies get from the campaigns alone. But it is my very strong opinion that all the pandering in all broadcast and print advertisements, empty promises, pontifications, mudslinging, and all the other vile political entertainment needs to be banned from the process. I am embarrassed and often wonder how the world views this. Imagine them all looking at how our leaders are torn down, ridiculed, lied about, and just about everything you can imagine. How embarrassing! We should all be ashamed.

Just present the facts: the candidates' track records, history of votes cast, and their future plans in each critical area of government. Prior to each debate, the candidate's position, in brief, on all facets of the American system should be read on air. Add up the cost of all the programs suggested and present a forecast to the American people of the actual cost of the ideas and recommendations of each candidate. This should be analyzed by independent, impartial groups. In addition, to educate voters, every American should be able to obtain a short fact sheet in the mail or at a local store or post office to see the résumé, track record, and a synopsis of each candidate's plan. This would make a huge difference in getting all of us the information we really need to vote wisely. However, if this were to occur, this would shake the very ground in Washington, because now the ignorant masses would be educated on the issues and see the candidates in black and white. That would be terrifying to DC.

The Several Hundred Million Dollar Election

I am appalled to hear politicians come out, time and time again, with ideas that I believe worsen our already-fragile economy and our country. But many Americans just eat it up and ask for seconds. Well, I am not buying one ounce of the slop being served to me about oil, the deficit, war, politics, China, mortgages, and what they think is good for my family and this country. Asking career public servants, academics, or politicians (most of whom have absolutely no experience) to solve an energy crisis, bank failures, and international problems is akin to throwing rocks at the sun. But even worse, they throw them at each other to make themselves look good.

If politicians want your opinion, they are happy to spend a few hundred million dollars to give it to you. So why do we buy into all this rhetoric and overlook their failure to execute the promises made during their campaign while they espouse ridiculous plans that we all know can't be feasible? Why do we just let it slide? Here is something refreshing. If I were ever running for office—but like most private sector people, I would never do so—the first words out of my mouth would be, "You know what I am going to promise the American People? NOTHING!" That's right, absolutely nothing. How can you stand before this nation and promise all these things if you have absolutely no idea what all the problems and issues are? You haven't even dug into the mess, and here you are pandering for votes again. You know only all too well that promises cost hundreds of billions of dollars, and you also know we are broke.

Unfortunately, the population is swayed by branding and excitement about the newest brands during each election cycle. Candidates become celebrities who are cheered for by zealots at huge rallies that are publicized all over television. They stand up on stages and perform like rock stars to stadiums full of fans. The press machines behind our politicians have done a far better job of using advertising and public relations than I have ever seen a private company do. We have been reduced to being consumers of political products and are fascinated by the entertainment value of political television. It's time we wake up to reality and realize that the government works for us! We have to raise the bar and insist on honesty, commonsense solutions, and an end to all the waste! You may not have had an appreciation for Ross Perot when he ran for president, but he was the first and only candidate I have ever seen pull out some charts and get hugely specific on his ideas. He spent hours and days of time and his own money to educate voters and present a business plan for a capitalist nation. Now that is what we should force all the panderers to do for us!

25

Read On

DO THE IDEAS, PLANS, programs, and solutions in this book seem reasonable to you? Did I mention that the government would *not* have to borrow any money to implement them?

Interesting, isn't it, that most private sector ideas for government never see the light of day, because by shedding light on these ideas, we pull the covers off of the broke, broken, and horrifying truth of how the government is handling our money and our future. To enact programs like these would gravely threaten the foundation of how our current system works, the people in power who run it, and the trillions of dollars being made by exploiting it. As radical as all this seems, I believe strongly that *if we do nothing, nothing will ever change.* But November is right around the corner.

In addition to the ideas presented in the previous chapters, I have some other radical ideas to share with you. Some are way out on the edge of a branch, but some may have a remote chance at happening. I am certain they will evoke other ideas from you and perhaps even entertain you as you think about them.

Hopefully this list will give you something to chew on, and perhaps some of the ideas will actually be seen by those decision makers and media personalities who can really make a difference.

Things America Must Do to Save Our Way of Life

As you know, the many things I have pointed out could never fix the horrifying way our country has been and is being run. Worse, there are so many other issues outside of our economy, healthcare, political machine, and path to destruction we are on that I need another guide to present them all, and that wouldn't be enough. I want to present a few here that I feel will fall on deaf political ears and such entrenched special interests and political machines that even considering them would be remote at best. But I will go for it anyway.

Energy

Did you know that more than 60 percent of the oil we use comes from Canada, the United States, and Latin America? We import most of our oil from Canada, and they hate us too! America needs to secure 100 percent of our natural resources from the United States, Canada, and Latin America where we can control the sources, cut Venezuela off completely, and shut down Citgo (Venezuela's government-owned gas business in the United States). For the record: 22 percent of our oil comes from Africa, over 12 percent from Europe, and only 18 percent from the Persian Gulf. Americans need to understand who is pulling the strings here, and it's not who we have been led to believe it is.

Solution 1: Drill Everywhere We Can. Alternative fuels will not be available for years, and the industry can't afford to shift overnight. This is a national security issue and should be treated like the Manhattan Project and Great Works programs. We need immediate, massive drilling and acquisition and exploration of natural gas and oil in America and everywhere overseas we can buy it. When I say massive drilling—I do mean utterly massive—how about using our own oil and natural gas production to pay off the debt? That is how Russia and Putin came to be so rich.

I know everyone is aware of this, and some support it and some don't. I want to see environmentalists stop driving their cars and boats anywhere and stop taking planes too! Go use a horse and buggy. Yes, we just had a massive spill in the Gulf of Mexico, but this should not deter us. We are just sitting here while China and Russia are buying up reserves all over the globe—very aggressively. Just watch Venezuelan president Hugo Chavez try to cut ties with nations across the world to halt its dependency on the United States for the sale of Venezuela's products and get us further over a barrel.

Solution 2: Coal. We have an almost infinite stockpile of coal. Get coal into all markets, industries, and any area that can use it. Gasification and liquid coal should be harnessed *immediately*. Clean coal technology is here *now* and can be an economic resurgence that is environmentally sound too. Yes, the recent coal mine tragedy was terrible and further sheds bad light on the industry, but coal powers a huge amount of our energy already. Want to go green—well, let's go black too.

Solution 3: Waste = "Trash to Cash." Use all waste facilities to put methane gas on the grid. We produce so much garbage that it can be a natural resource if managed properly. Waste Management Inc. is making huge strides in this area, and we should incentivize the whole refuse industry.

Solution 4: Natural Gas. There is an abundant supply of natural gas right here at home. Although industries and automobiles would take a while to convert, America should begin retooling its industries to use natural gas as a predominant source of energy and to send a message to the rest of the world. This will take time to implement, but with huge stockpiles of it here at home, we should be going blue too. I am black, blue, and green in the face about this!

Solution 5: Alternative Energy. We should continue to invest in wind power, solar energy, fuel cells, and all other energy sources. Again, this will take time, but it should be the most massive investment strategy ever undertaken by America. Taking a page from the information age—it was led initially by the government—the Defense Advanced Research Projects Agency (DARPA) and the defense industry created the Internet, then called ARPANET, and it was led by scientists at Bolt Beranek & Newman (BB&N) in Cambridge, Massachusetts. We need to unleash the giant. Look at how Silicon Valley drove the technology and information revolution. There is so much inaction, lack or urgency, stagnation, and red tape in DC that the many things we need to do just crawl like a snail through Congress while China has a massive sense of urgency on all fronts. We need to use every tool in the shed! If the investment the government is making was given to venture capitalists, there would be an utterly massive revolution in alternative energy science and solutions. But again, politicians can't get out of our way—and of course their own.

Solution 6: Nuclear Energy. Well, what a mistake. In the 1970s the very groups that helped thwart the large-scale nuclear buildout for energy in the United States are the ones eating their words. As long as we can secure the facilities like military installations from the crazies, I say, "Go Large." You want to get people back to work, then kill two birds. Instead of extending unemployment benefits and such, take billions and embark on a Panama Canal–like project! What on earth are we are waiting for? However, as with anything led by the government, it is so backward and caught up in a mess, who knows when it may start and how slow it will be.

Immigration and Borders

This country was founded on the principle of an open door for anyone wanting to come here to find freedom. Well, don't you think it's time to change this policy? Our nation is overrun with illegal aliens. I understand their value to our economy and the fact that jobs performed by illegal aliens are those many Americans will not or don't want to do. But we are already an entitlement nation, and we are entitling these non-Americans to do jobs that people on unemployment or welfare should be doing. If you don't like working part time doing these hard jobs while we pay you, then too bad. If you want a check, then work for it!

Solution 1: The Great Wall of America. Immediately build a wall around this country. If we can build the Hoover Dam, the Panama Canal, and other great projects that created thousands of jobs, why can't we employ tens of thousands of Americans to build the Great Wall of America? In an age of global terrorism and asymmetric technology (meaning people across the globe have access to powerful technology once controlled by governments), it is never more necessary to seal our borders tightly. Another way is to build an electrified fence across the nation. Let's see someone try to cut a hole in that! I know people will try to dig tunnels underneath and pile into trucks and buses to get here, but if we can detect a snake moving around Area 51, then we should be able to supplement the border wall with technology to thwart trespassing and install x-ray technology at every border crossing to root out illegals and also potentially catastrophic materials from entering our nation in cars and trucks.

Solution 2: Round Up the Illegals. Why should America be burdened with an entire class of people that isn't paying taxes or on the way to citizenship? I want to gather up all illegal aliens in this country and give them one shot at becoming an American citizen, but they'd be required to go to the end of the line, behind the others who have already applied legally. Any illegal caught after the amnesty would be immediately deported. This would take a herculean effort in all major cities and towns, but the task would employ potentially tens of thousands of Americans! We could use the National Guard while on duty and the domestic military force to supplement the police and the newly created work force (jobs). This is and has been a politically uncomfortable subject, but why? Get them out of here! I really can't believe there is even talk about this. Yes, many are good, hardworking, and very respectable people who just want a chance at a better life. But they need to go to the back of the bus. Gang members, freeloaders, criminals, killers, rapists, and the lazy should be rounded up and thrown back over the wall. Unfortunately, no political party wants to lose Hispanic votes come election time, so we continue to tip-toe around the issue.

Solution 3: Free Trade Creates a Porous Border. Free-trade programs with Canada and Mexico allow traffic to flow seamlessly in and out of the United States. I believe that anyone involved in commerce from Canada and Mexico must have a valid, bar-coded ID to enter America that is actually enforceable and not able to be replicated. Also, any individual wanting to come across the border must have a similar ID or be denied access. The pass can be manually checked or electronically scanned at the border—preferably electronically to save money. Since there would be a database, every person coming into the country would be accounted for, and we could check patterns, frequency, time spent, etc. to analyze and track everyone as they move through and around the country. We do not want to impede trade, and God forbid we should get in the way of making a buck, but I assure you someone or something will come across the border from Mexico or Canada and wreak massive havoc on our nation. In fact, I am certain that dangerous people and terrorists already have used these routes to get in here. Our systems are woefully inadequate, and we continue to throw people and billions at the problem, and it still gets worse year after year.

Solution 4: Illegal Alien Martial Law. For a period of time, martial law needs to be imposed in our cities and towns while we extract the illegal aliens. Anyone without proof of citizenship or carrying a work permit or green card will be rounded up and deported. Our police, National Guard, and military should be assigned to root out these people and send them on their way. If we really wanted to solve gang violence, drug problems, illegal aliens, and such, we would declare martial law and go get them all. But I assure you that no one in DC would ever take the risk of even saying this, although it would one the best things America could do for itself.

Terrorism

There is nothing more dangerous to our culture than the continued weaponization of science and the dissemination of intellectual property in the form of technology and people. If terrorists or rogue nations possess this technology and know-how, we are in *big* trouble. Nuclear and chemical weapons are dangerous enough, but as terrifying as the prospect that these may make it to our shores and be used, this still represents what I call a finite event. By no means am I discounting loss of life and devastation, but the result would be isolated to a specific area. A thousand times worse and easier to smuggle into our country or other countries are biological and molecular weapons. If you have seen the movie *12 Monkeys* or *Outbreak* (if not, rent them), you have seen that these types of weapons represent a human species impact.

Unfortunately, the United States is a target that will be struck again and again. Random bombings and large-scale attacks are only the beginning. As technology continues to surpass our humanity, nations and radicals want to wield the hand of God against our nation, even if the result is a threat to the survival of the human race. I don't think the public is aware or keeps this inevitable fact on the front burner. Like the financial crisis, the United States is geared only to react to the next attack.

Terrorists lurk around every corner and are all over the world. They, too, use the media to promote their exploits and causes, and they know it is the most powerful weapon out there for them to use. The enemy is largely hidden and faceless, which is the main problem when our goal is to find them and kill them. A central command doesn't exist, nor even a clear battleground where we can engage the enemy. Iraq and Afghanistan have created fronts and battlefields, so we can lure the enemy out of the caves and the mountains and the jungles to fight us. Iraq became a major front for the war on terror. The front is very necessary, or we will be hunting in the dark instead of creating a vacuum to suck them into a fight. These wars formed a battleground overseas to fight terrorists, and believe me, it's definitely better fought over there than here in America.

Solution 1: Avoid Another Vietnam. Once again the politicians are running wars. This is reminiscent of the Vietnam War, when we couldn't go into Laos or Cambodia to hunt our enemy. If our enemy is emboldened and is resident in a foreign nation, we should seek permission to attack massively. If permission isn't granted, we need to take matters into our own hands. War is war. Period! If our enemy is hiding behind a cloak of political refuge or sovereignty—and laughing at us—then all bets are off.

Pakistan is a great example of where we must interdict and wipe out the support structure of al Qaeda and the Taliban. These lawless tribal areas in northern Pakistan where the Taliban is hiding are tip-toed around like tulips. We have to sneak in and kill a few at a time, while they march closer and closer toward Islamabad with the potential of turning the Pakistani nuclear nation upside down. I did say *nuclear!* What we need is a problem eradicator, not some armchair politician trying to win points and votes, but someone who will use military force the likes of which the world has never seen. We need to bomb into rubble any and every area where these groups are hiding.

Solution 2: Take Off the Velvet Gloves. Let our military fight a war like it should be fought. We have become political warriors and police. Do you think the radicals of other nations that attack us would be so kind? Do you think they'd hesitate to behead us? Do you believe they would be putting people on trial? We know too well what these people think of women. What do think they would do to women in modern culture, and can you imagine what is happening to women and children in northern Pakistan and southern Afghanistan? How about torture? Do you think they wouldn't and don't torture! And here we are putting Navy Seals and the CIA on trial for getting the requisite intelligence out of these murderers. Scalp them, pull their fingernails and teeth out, drown them, beat them, or use whatever means is necessary, because they would definitely not hesitate for a moment to do it to us. In fact, if they get captured, they know how we will treat them and the mild way we will deal with them. We need to bring the wrath of God upon them and scare them to their core so they will cough up the information we need to save American lives.

Mark my words: in war, the most committed side wins, and the only thing respected in this world is *power.* If our enemy loves death and we love life, then we are already on the wrong side of war. If our enemy is willing to behead people and chop off hands without a second thought, then we have a big problem, because they are more committed to victory than we are and will use any and every means to win. They have no political consequences to hold them back. I believe that if America is terrorized, the United States should go in *with all guns blazing* and utterly crush our enemies and even the nations from where these people operate. But politicians are running our wars again, and our military has to be shot at first before our soldiers can engage the enemy. That is outrageous! These people are assassinating, blowing themselves up, jumping out from behind walls and everything else under the sun, and smashing our own planes into economic and military (and maybe political) centers of our country. Unfortunately, I think a majority of fickle Americans have placed the memories of 9/11 somewhere in the back of their minds.

Unleash hell upon them! Or as Shakespeare said so eloquently, "Cry havoc, and let slip the dogs of war!" In this case, *havoc* was a signal given to the English generals during the Middle Ages to direct the soldiery to pillage and plunder the enemy.

Solution 3: Put a $10 Billion Bounty on the Heads of the Leaders of Rogue Nations. We pay so much for war against the nations and their armies that are commanded by individuals. The money could be better used to have everyone in the world incentivized to find and kill these leaders.

See if that kind of money doesn't offer an incentive to the people to overthrow or kill these murderers, and heck, it'll save a lot of lives and money. Although millions of dollars have been allotted to capture or even kill terrorists like Osama Bin Laden, no one is going after the heads of other nations. Even in the terrorism cases, we can certainly boost the incentive so every gun-carrying person on earth will be after them. I am sure that for a few billion dollars someone will come home with a scalp.

Solution 4: Bring Our Troops Home from Bases Around the World—But Keep Air and Naval Power Deployed. If we can quickly exert power anywhere, then why should we have all of our troops stationed all over the globe? Never divide your forces. Get these troops back here to rebuild America, police our streets, and protect our borders. Now doesn't that make sense? We need to start looking out for our own, and with our first responders and police so overburdened, we could use every asset in our arsenal. By the way, don't you hear those nations griping and groaning about us being there already! We spend huge sums of money in those nations, and our soldiers are a critical part of their economy. Bye-bye! Get them home and spend the money here. Then watch the tears in the eyes of all those who are casting stones at us.

Welfare Country

We are no longer a working nation; we have become an entitlement nation. Many people think they are owed something just because they breathe American air. This is socialism, and the media dances around this, but I assure you our nation is going down the socialist path. In fact, we are about to hugely penalize Americans who make good money and even the rich—those who employ most everyone else—and give it away to people who we all know sit around and moan and groan that they aren't getting enough. America owes them. Blah, blah, blah. I'm sick of it. The redistribution of wealth in a capitalist nation is obscene; in fact, doing just that is the root of communism and socialism. However, socialism is a great way to keep people kneeling at the government altar and bowing to the political elite through the ballot box. Liberal government continues to harness more power, even more than capitalism is designed to foster, and there has never been a society or empire in history that has survived because it has gone down the path of liberalism. History repeats!

Solution 1: Work. Anyone on welfare, food stamps, or other forms of government handouts must work at least twenty hours a week performing some civic duty. They can help build the Great Wall of America or clean up the parks and streets. Whatever area has a need, these people must work or risk being removed from government programs. We pay them, why not put them to work?

Solution 2: New Skills. Anyone on welfare or participating in other government assistance programs must attend a work program fifteen hours per week to learn new skills and increase his or her education. We have to provide hope for people that need it, so they can have a fighting chance beyond just handing them money.

Solution 3: Drug Screening. Anyone being subsidized must submit to drug screenings. This is an absolute. Drug and alcohol abuse is a driver for unproductivity. Certainly not everyone living off of or relying on the government uses drugs or abuses alcohol, but if we want to clean up the streets and get people back on their feet, then we had better root out the bad apples and get them help so they can have a fighting chance and not be perpetually dependent on the government.

Solution 4: Child Education. Any parents on welfare or participating in other government assistance programs must have their children attend an educational program, especially early education, or risk being expelled from government programs. This is a huge problem. Most of the poor have no hope at all. Many young Americans find their lives revolving around their neighborhood and getting drawn into fast bucks and gangs. How can we ever fix the problem if we are not trying to promote them out of poverty? Of course they may not be thrilled at having to work and go to school. But this would free up their time to do the things that get them on a positive track while the children get a fighting chance and head start. With all the waste in our system, people falling through the cracks and getting a hand out is the biggest waste of all. I am not advocating another government program here. The commercial sector can take the reins and create a very efficient and effective means to get these children into programs (for example, Sylvan learning) that will open their eyes to many possibilities instead of just leaving them behind.

Culture

Our culture has become decadent, weak, and, frankly, a mess. From Aquarius to hip-hop, the musical decades correlate closely to our social disintegration. The complete breakdown of the family and the rise of gang violence, hopelessness, poor education, and a myriad of other issues have torn our social fabric to shreds. There was a time when every American stood up for every other American. For a while after 9/11, we all banded together as Americans, but that only lasted a short while.

In fact, Maslow's hierarchy of needs in many places in

America is so upside down that food, shelter, and love are out of reach. Just walking home from school, children are exposed to drive-by shootings, murder, drug deals, and gangs. What kind of adults will these children become? One of their hierarchy of needs may be to just to get home safe from school. It is horrifying, and we all see it right in front of us, or we know about it and turn a blind eye. Our cultural decay is epidemic. I look back to the 1950s, and I can guarantee you that the purity of that time in our history is lost forever. Imagine back then widespread pornography, hip-hop culture, gang violence as it is today, today's television programming, and on and on. It would be unheard of, but at that time in our history we were the strongest, and when history writes about the American Empire, they will look back to the time just after World War II and measure the decay or our society from there. It is a slippery slope, and we aren't even running uphill anymore; we have already fallen and are sliding down the hill and fast approaching the cliff that awaits us.

Solution 1: Mandated Service Programs. All kids at age eighteen must spend one year in an America-focused Peace Corps, the military, the National Guard, or another social works program without pay. Housing, clothes, and food would be provided. The kids can also stay one additional year if they want a head start in a state college by working for the state in which they reside. On-the-job training and skills can be taught, and kids will be taken off the streets and given an opportunity to turn their lives around and enhance their commitment to America. This league can be used in many ways to help rebuild America and to instill morals and rebuild the character of our next generation. This alone would have a huge impact on our nation and for generations to come.

Solution 2: Community Service. All kids in high school must spend ten hours a week providing community service. This works program can be established for mandated credits so that their contribution to the community can be monitored, measured, and recognized by their school. Any proceeds from the work would be paid back to the school they are attending. This would be another way to create revenue for schools.

Solution 3: Mentoring System. Elderly to middle-aged, middle-aged to adult, adult to teen, teen on down, through every age group in school and society should be involved in a mentoring program. Although it may not be possible across adult society, a mandate that children of every age in school should be responsible for a child one grade below them would be a powerful boon to the country. Help Americans to help other Americans and pass down the fundamentals for living a better life. I am sure the bullying headlines would be greatly reduced if we are all looking out for one another.

Solution 4: Wisdom Classes in Grade School, High School, and College. Kids should take life lessons from the elderly and the terminally ill. We should create course work for our children to learn about the principles that are most important in life. Having these people speak and mentor others would have a profound impact on people of all ages. The elderly and the sick can also feel a sense of renewed purpose to try to change even one life. Just think how valuable this would be to have younger people see the other side of life. The perspective they gain would be superior to many of the useless typing and study hall hours spent in school.

Solution 5: Empower the FCC to Halt All Vile Programming That Can Reach Our Children. The government should mandate that all satellite providers and all cable companies provide a free package that includes only family-friendly content. Take all urban gang and violent programming out of public music and television programming. This, more than anything, would reach our children and eliminate huge issues for the next generation. Somehow our nation needs to conclude that free speech is essential, but free speech that denigrates society in the most public ways and massively influences bad behavior and violence is not acceptable. People will challenge this and fight it all the way to the Supreme Court, and this idea will get shot down. But what does it say about our Constitution when the very things we hold sacred are leveraged to spread and glorify hate, violence, wild sex, drinking, drug use, and so many antisocial behaviors. What is wrong with us? Do we really think our Founding Fathers had this in mind when they talked about free speech?

Solution 6: Gang and Urban Violence. Since the gang segment of our society has been glorified to our younger generation, this issue needs to be cleaned up in a huge way. All gang members, urban bullies, and would-be criminals need to be sent to boot camp. The National Guard, police, and military should be tasked with patrolling every city and collecting all people and unregistered arms that are part of organized gangs or other violent cliques. Reeducation can get these people off the streets, clean them up, wean them off drugs, offer them a two-year education, and condition them to be contributing members of society. During their tenure they would perform work that impacts their community or the nation. This would be a massive undertaking: Operation Clean Sweep. What we need is a broom and dustpan to scrape up all these people. You think martial law is out of the question? It is exactly what we need to clean ourselves up, but I am certain that no politician has the guts to propose such a radical program.

Prisons

America's prisons have become educational institutions for professional criminals. Offenders go to prison and network with other prisoners, learn the criminal craft, and get raped, killed, or beaten. How do you think these people will return to society? As better criminals! No wonder recidivism (the repeat offenders that go in and out of jail) is so high. Ah, but I have a great solution for this problem too!

Solution 1: Export Our Prisons. Why should hardworking taxpayers finance these offenders and their comforts? I propose we create a great economy for Mexico, Africa, or other nations that need the revenue. Why do we build and run these prisons here when we can save billions by moving them to other nations that can do it cheaper? Well, here we go again with earmarks, and even bigger are the population counts of prisoners for redistricting and state and federal funding. Why should anyone pay for this and even let them be counted for political gain.

Solution 2: Lose Citizenship—The American Gulag. Commit a crime deemed worthy of losing your citizenship, and you go to Greenland or Antarctica. Your citizenship would be immediately revoked if you're found guilty and you will be exiled. Let's see how many gang bangers, child molesters, murderers, and rapists want to get kicked out and sent to a cold, barren wasteland. Why should they get three squares a day, a quiet cell, free books, free television, free time, covert drugs, gay sex, and so forth. Kick these people out of here! They are just taking up our money and have no useful purpose in our society.

Solution 3: Forfeit Rights. When someone enters the prison system today, they have all of their rights protected and are treated to a life that isn't too bad: three meals a day, friends, television, books, drugs, and sex. The victims, on the other hand, have nothing but pain and loss, and many have no life at all after it was taken by a criminal. Yet we give these criminals rights! Take away all their rights and privileges. How? Lock down the prisons. Lock the prisoners in cells for twenty-three hours a day and let them out cell block by cell block for an hour a day. Feed prisoners in their cells, and only reward those who participate in a work or education program if they are allowed to. Some prisons do just that, and you see all the sob stories on television or hear of people going crazy and climbing the walls. Hey, here is a suggestion: go overseas and take a tour of some of those prisons. You think those people have all the comforts that we afford? Let them rot in there, especially those who have committed terrible crimes or are lifers. For certain crimes and those that can prove themselves, just maybe they will get an opportunity to work for society or, better yet, their victims.

Solution 4: Forfeit Assets. Criminals committing certain crimes should be stripped of all their assets. All assets should immediately go to their victims. The prisoners must then work for the rest of their time in prisons, and all their proceeds should go to the families they harmed. Today, they work cheaply for companies that use prison labor. That is crazy! Criminals should be working for their victims.

CONCLUSION

I HAVE PAINTED A grim picture of this nation's woes. But for two years I have also run my observations and ideas past dozens of influential businesspeople, civilians, and tens of thousands across the radio airwaves with overwhelming concurrence, although some of the ideas are too far out on a limb. When I hear the talking points on the nation's airwaves today, I am comforted that perhaps I was on the right track when most of this was written. I believe there are economic solutions to America's issues, and we must be tenacious in pursuing them, because this economic disaster is our gravest threat. In this book, I have also included some social issues, which represent just a small percentage of America's problems. It is my hope that after reading this book you will be more informed and more motivated to enact change in our country. Everyone must do his or her part. We're all in this together! I hope you will get the word out to everyone you know, because we must be heard or we will continue to live in quiet desperation while our nation is squandered before our eyes. Again, NOVEMBER IS AROUND THE CORNER!

We all know that Washington DC has to be sanitized, but nothing ever changes. We all know this country is essentially bankrupt, but we allow the downward spiral to continue. We all see corruption, violence, and bad news on television every night. But we are all convinced that we have no power to change anything, so we just consume what they serve us. And so the wheels of this nation just spin and spin, and there is no stopping us from going over Capitol Cliff (not Capitol Hill).

The power to change this country lies in the microphone, on television, and in print media and books. The only way to get the word out and inspire this nation is through the media. And I know that together we have enough of a voice to put the real issues on the table and get the government to listen. Just look at all the attention the Tea Party movement is getting! If you are in that movement, please pass this along to whoever will shout the loudest.

ABOUT THE AUTHOR

BILL GLYNN, "A Think Tank of One," has been a venture capitalist and entrepreneur for twenty years and is the author of *Left on Red* and *The United States of Bankruptcy.* He was ranked by Information Week as one of fifteen top innovators globally. He is an insider in the film and music industry. The companies he has founded, helped build, and invested in have raised over one billion dollars (iChat, How Stuff Works, Red Storm Entertainment—Tom Clancy Games, to mention a few). Bill advises Fortune 1000 companies and select emerging businesses, and he often turns his ideas into entrepreneurial success stories. He is a supporter of various nongovernmental organizations with an eye toward harmonizing humanity across the major religions and the weaponization of science. He served his country in the U.S. Air Force.

Bill is a regular public speaker and appears on radio shows from coast to coast, reaching millions of listeners every month.

You may read more about Bill or contact him at his Web site, www.billyg.net.